**Ma(r)king Ground: Three Projects**
by Ada Karmi-Melamede

**For my brother Ram Karmi**

**F**

FRANCES LINCOLN LIMITED
PUBLISHERS

**Ma(r)king Ground: Three Projects**
by Ada Karmi-Melamede

Frances Lincoln Ltd
74–77 White Lion Street
London N1 9PF
www.franceslincoln.com

Published with the support of Yad Hanadiv
(The Rothschild Foundation)

Copyright © Ada Karmi-Melamede 2013

First Frances Lincoln edition 2013

All rights reserved. No part of this publication may be reproduced, stored in a retrieval system or transmitted in any form, or by any means, electronic, mechanical, photocopying, recording or otherwise, without either permission in writing from the publisher or a licence permitting restricted copying. In the United Kingdom such licences are issued by the Copyright Licensing Agency, Saffron House, 6–10 Kirby Street, London EC1N 8TS.

A catalogue record for this book is available from the British Library.

ISBN 978-0-7112-3463-5

Printed in China

9 8 7 6 5 4 3 2 1

Graphic design: Gila Kaplan, Nirit Binyamini
Editing: Ada Karmi Melamede & Guy Teomi
Production editor: Michael Brunström
Photography: Richard Bryant, Ardon Bar-Hama, Amit Geron

**Ma(r)king Ground: Three Projects**
by Ada Karmi-Melamede

| | |
|---|---|
| **1** | **Preface** |
| **4** | **Essay: Ma(r)king Ground: Three Projects by Ada Karmi-Melamede** / Raymund Ryan |
| **10** | **The Visitors Centre – Ramat Hanadiv** |
| **40** | **The Open University – Ra'anana** |
| **80** | **The Supreme Court – Jerusalem** |
| **126** | **Epilogue** |
| **128** | **Credits** |

# Ma(r)king Ground: Three Projects
by Ada Karmi-Melamede
----
Raymund Ryan

The term 'architect' has in recent years appeared in hitherto unlikely places. Politicians are 'architects' of economical and military strategies. Civil servants are 'architects', we are led to believe, of complex bureaucratic machinations. And media types from Madison Avenue to Hollywood are 'architects' of campaigns to promote, sell and disseminate this or that desirable product. Yet this complicated, globalized, often fickle world still has architects in the core, essential sense of that word. One of these is Ada Karmi-Melamede. Karmi-Melamede is a real architect.

A real architect today needs to steer an independent course between, on one hand, a certain demoralization at redefinitions and expectations of the profession of architecture and, on the other, a kind of zany euphoria instigated by beguiling new technologies and by what Guy Debord critically termed *The Society of the Spectacle*. Amid these competing and confusing claims for attention, Karmi-Melamede stands her ground. Furthermore, we might even say that she makes her ground, or the ground of her architecture, as each project, while satisfying a need for space, also makes place.

This is another key binary in an understanding of contemporary architecture: the push-and-pull between abstract spatial organization and a social, cultural, perhaps even psychological need for place, a sense of where we are.

Modernism produced buildings often divorced from the physical, historical and ecological potential of site. Modernism succeeded in Europe after the First World War with the promise not merely of functionalism – of rational construction and programmatic analysis – but of a better, more equal society. In the 1950s, Corporate Modernism, from New York to Brasilia, both beguiled and alienated the public, with standalone boxes for Big Business and Big Government. While a subsequent generation, in the 1980s, exaggerated figuration and quotation in attempts to give architecture legibility and meaning, architects today are faced with increasingly urgent issues of sustainability and the proper use of resources.

The work of Ada Karmi-Melamede embodies her careful assimilation and critique of such major trends in progressive world architecture. This has nothing to do with fashion or theoretical gamesmanship. In her work one recognizes instead a Modernist pleasure in the plan, in structure and in circulation. There is a calibration of components and of systems designed to be experienced through movement, as envisaged by Le Corbusier with the *promenade architecturale*. Karmi-Melamede is also deeply conscious of the role of institutions in democratic society. The purpose or goal of her work shares a profound affinity, in this regard, with Louis Kahn's almost gnomic pronouncements in post-War America.

Three recent buildings by Karmi-Melamede, all with the active support of Yad Hanadiv (the Rothschild Foundation) – the Supreme Court (with Ram Karmi), the Open University, and a visitors centre at Ramat Hanadiv – seem induced from, as much as imposed upon, their three distinct terrains. Each in its own way fosters gathering.

The Supreme Court of Israel is the most public example of these humanistic concerns. This building, or more correctly this complex of buildings, negotiates its presence on a gentle rise through a series of alignments, shifts in section, the creation of outdoor rooms (and of internal spaces that feel almost like outdoor rooms), and the punctuation of its roofscape to allow natural light a specific role in our exploration of the interior. It is both a monument representing the State and its people and a cluster of village- or villa-like components in which the institution's users may feel at home. Designed in partnership with Karmi-Melamede's older brother, Ram, himself a distinguished Modernist architect, the Supreme Court is also an essay in the use of stone.

On the plains between Jerusalem and the sea, Ra'anana is less redolent of history, more representative of where Israelis live and work today. There the Open University occupies an elongated site between a motorway and a new apartment precinct. Although the campus planned by Karmi-Melamede is not yet complete, the idea is clear. It is framed by a phalanx of cubic buildings, opposite the apartments, and a linear edifice parallel to the motorway. Together they help define a long, triangular garden from which motor traffic is removed. The cubic buildings crank open to direct circulation and instigate views, and are hollowed out to make patios. There is again an invitation to explore and here we notice, more evident than at the Supreme Court, the coexistence of stone carapace and bones of concrete.

In northern Israel, Ramat Hanadiv holds a special role in the nation's culture. On a hilltop within a nature reserve is a lush garden with distant views to the Mediterranean. The garden is an elegant memorial to the Rothschild family – Baron Edmond de Rothschild, 'The Benefactor', and his wife are buried on the grounds. Nevertheless, the ambience is not mournful. Our first impression is rather of fresh air, the values of nature and of scientific cultivation. Karmi-Melamede's building here is almost no building at all. It's a kind of artificial dune between the car park and the formal gateway, a linear topology split and pried apart to facilitate circulation and illumination. It seems to emerge from the ground (stone walls, grass roof) and be protective rather than overtly rhetorical.

These three projects – law court, university, garden – vary in scale and location within Israel. Nevertheless there are distinct and distinctive qualities common to Karmi-Melamede's work. These qualities are forged from the architect's attention to site and from her meticulous working through design and construction stages to arrive at an architecture that is sober, elegant, and intended for the greater public good.

**From Ground to Light**

In all three cases, the architecture of Ada Karmi-Melamede gives priority to the land. Her buildings nestle into the topography or harness differences in level so that the starting point for construction is never a *tabula rasa*, that hypothetical blank slate of so many Modernist projects. This is key to her practice, her reworking of the twentieth-century canon to incorporate the ground beneath a building as well as the air above. This strategy is in part pragmatic: building sites, even on flat land, are excavated to lay foundations and, especially in urban situations, to embed basements and underground car parks. The seamless flat plaza beneath many a Modernist tower is thus often a costly illusion.

As phenomenological philosophers such as Gaston Bachelard have noted, ascending and descending within built structures trigger associations in the human mind, associations that both guide us from A to B and help establish memory or sense of place. Karmi-Melamede is not obsessed with lower levels *per se*. Her interest is in the entire architectural structure. Her buildings emerge out of the earth – Ramat Hanadiv appearing barely at all. They fracture the earth's crust and make protective precincts, such as those around several houses by Karmi-Melamede and the great sunken garden at the Supreme Court. The façades of her buildings are subsequent to and largely determined by such priorities.

Ramat Hanadiv and the Supreme Court are of course scenographic, their designs calibrated to avail of and augment their specific locations and landscapes. Conversely, the Open University fabricates its topography, establishing physical boundaries and manipulating the ground plane to cognitive and experiential effect. [1] Hence the long linear path running inside the propped colonnade and descending in gentle steps as it nears the principal courtyard of the university.

The site for the Supreme Court is not simply any plot of land. It's a unique site between the Knesset and the Crowne Plaza tower, with the Old City to the east and an array of government ministries and the Israel Museum to the west. The Karmis designed this latest critical facility as a crossroads, as the intersection of routes linking these other key agents of the modern state, such that everyday users of the building and its many public visitors experience the interconnectivity of these institutions through circulation and views. [2] Moreover, the marking of the ground by the axial promenade leading to the Knesset, crossed and overlaid by the great arc of a curving stone wall, apportion quadrants of the precinct to distinct programs – courtrooms, offices, library, and underground parking.

The Supreme Court might thus be thought of an earthwork with characteristics of both Land Art sculpture and an archaeological dig. In the 1970s and early 1980s, Michael Heizer's *Double Negative* on a mesa north of Las Vegas, Maya Lin's *Vietnam Veterans Memorial* in Washington D.C., and several hypothetical projects by the Argentinian visionary Emilio Ambasz fused professional categorizations of art, landscape architecture and architectural design. Ramat Hanadiv is the closest in intention to these essentially minimalist designs. Karmi-Melamede classifies her intervention there as 'a building along a route'. She envisioned the structure in harmony with nature's contours such that, from outside, it does not appear as a building in any obvious sense. [3]

The Supreme Court is less minimalist, more complicated and filled with incident; it may even evoke the ludic complexity of the villa built millennia ago by Emperor Hadrian on the outskirts of Rome. This necessity in Jerusalem today is due to the multiplicity of parts required by the programme and by a need to lead visitors through the halls and chambers and passageways by providing architectural clues, as if in a splendid democratic labyrinth. At the Supreme Court, we encounter architecture not only as form but as information. Critical shapes and spaces (positives and negatives) recall known prototypes – the pyramidal roof of the library lobby seems to channel, for example, the ancient and hollow Tomb of Absalom at Kidron. [4]

If the Supreme Court conjures known typologies and historical allusion, this is due not only to the period during which it was designed but also to the inherent institutional need to communicate purpose and reason for being. It is literally and figuratively a palimpsest, a composition of layers. Such striation of vertical and horizontal surfaces results from decisions within the construction process yet also evoke a sense of culture and the strategic accumulation of knowledge over decades and centuries of architectural proposition, building use, and design refinement. The stratification in section also acts to isolate the paths of defendants, judges, and lay visitors.

Karmi-Melamede's use of stone clearly signals a respect for historical precedence, for local craft, and for indigenous materials. At the Supreme Court and at Ramat Hanadiv, the stone has mass and feels heavy as if the new spaces have been excavated or carved from the earth. Whereas the interior of the Court is characterized by brilliant, light-reflecting white plaster, the robust exterior with its massive ashlar corners reinterprets or recalls the ancient city walls close by. [5] At the Open University, however, stone and concrete visibly co-exist. Less prescribed by context, the university is more conscious perhaps of looking to the future and a correspondingly appropriate tectonic language. Concrete is proudly exposed for much of the exterior whereas stone wraps and lines the internal façades. Stone – Israeli stone in all three cases, quarried in the Negev – is evocative not only of patrimony but has also an immediate affinity with our human senses. It provides texture and welcomes daylight much as our own skins do after periods of darkness or hibernation.

Whether load-bearing, as in traditional construction, or applied as membrane to a structural frame, stone wraps space in attractive, haptic ways. This is particularly true when light and shadow are in play, as here in Israel. Without its rich lining of stone, the sequence of chambers at Ramat Hanadiv would risk a certain clinical detachment or mundane abstraction. The stone reinforces our sense of being within, and together with, the earth, an emotion animated by the controlled admission of sunlight, by the apparent softening of stone by this filigree of light, and by the patterning of walls and floors by light and shadow. [6] Sunlight is a timeless and completely free material, needing only its orchestration by a sensitive designer.

Within Modernism, many architects looked to ancient and non-Western buildings for inspiration. Louis Kahn's almost childlike drawings caught the massive ruins at Karnak and Paestum dematerialising in light; whereas Le Corbusier, who travelled to Constantinople as early as 1911, famously promoted architecture as 'the masterly, correct, and magnificent play of volumes brought together in light'. It is this attention to light – so vital yet also potentially devastating in the Israeli climate – that enlivens the massive, at times monolithic, interiors of stone and concrete realized by Ada Karmi-Melamede. In this period of stylistic uncertainly, her buildings emerge from the ground – literally and metaphorically – towards controlled islands of sunlight.

## Geometry in the Service of Architecture

The Kahnian wall – sturdy and timeless and waiting to be blessed by light – is present in Karmi-Melamede's work. There is also Kahnian fragmentation, a strategy that has led in other architects' work to overt eclecticism, but that is stabilized here through rigorous geometries and a judicious palette of materials. Le Corbusier's poetic logic is echoed in the balancing of forms, both solid and void (drum, cube, pyramid), and the interconnective tissue of corridors, staircases, hallways, and framed views.

These lessons from the Swiss–French master seem filtered through the example of such English Modernists as James Stirling (both Karmis studied at London's Architectural Association in the 1950s) and the re-codification of Le Corbusier's work by a New York avant garde, including Richard Meier in the 1960s and 1970s. In this regard, the Supreme Court shares a post-Corbusian cluster sensibility with Meier's contemporary Getty Center in Los Angeles; yet whereas the Getty uses its hilltop site as a splendid private terrace, the Court directly engages its location and topography, hollowing out a set of surprisingly accessible rooms, gardens and passageways.

Le Corbusier titled one section of his seminal 1923 book *Towards a New Architecture*, 'The Exterior is Always an Interior'. That message is doubly true at the Open University. The primary form frames a triangular interior court protected from the outer world and skewered by paths that skip across a garden that will slope, in turn, in the opposite direction – to an amphitheatre still to be realized. This is the main exterior room. The larger buildings along the southern boundary are, however, also hollow. These palazzo-scaled structures splay open to reveal subsidiary patios nesting within, reminiscent of outdoor quads at residential Oxbridge and Ivy League colleges. Each, invariably, is an implied square in plan.

One can in fact search with pleasure through Karmi-Melamede's plans for squares or partial squares, from the large gesture of the roof of the parking structure at the Supreme Court (punctured by a circular opening) to the double-storey restaurant pavilion at the terminus of the promenade running through the linear berm at Ramat Hanadiv. Square rooms inside the Court include the aedicule porch facing the Knesset, the Chief Justice's office in the prow of the judges' private chambers, and the base of the pyramid that signals the library. At Ramat Hanadiv, the satellite office building [7] is a kind of broken square doughnut, recalling in this regard several buildings by the Finnish Modernist, Alvar Aalto, which combine the certainty of geometry with a fragmentary aspect open to nature.

At the Supreme Court, Karmi-Melamede, in collaboration with her brother Ram, also introduces circles and semicircles. Notice the singular oculus above each courtroom; the balconies projecting from the judge's chambers; the vertical north portal with its suggestions of a fortress gateway; and the beautifully detailed, inverted ziggurat of the law library. That remarkable space, lit by clerestory windows circling the base of the copper-clad pyramid, is one of several special volumes inserted into the architectural mass as fine-tuned vessels. Similarly, at the Open University, a quarter-circle pavilion houses an intimate synagogue that is focused on a trunk of vertical timber slats rising to splay out as a concentric fan. The trunk protects the holy ark whereas the canopy above screens interior lighting equipment. [8]

Because this is Israel, these squares, circles and triangles may be external or internal, enclosed or open to the sky.

The architect has absorbed the Modernist premise of unobstructed space flowing freely between interior and exterior; yet she has also thoroughly studied local historic architecture, so often punctured to dramatically admit narrow shafts of light. The sky is frequently the ceiling of the most memorable rooms in these sophisticated structures, as at the long patio surrounded by judges' offices at the Supreme Court [9], inspired – as Karmi-Melamede readily admits – by the pristine courtyard of the Rockefeller Museum designed during the British Mandate period, in the 1920s, by Austen St Barbe Harrison. That courtyard, in turn, was inspired by the famed patios of the Alhambra in Granada, Spain, patios at once delicate and monolithic and that represent an apogee in Islamic and Mediterranean design.

If the sky-as-ceiling is literally paramount, as with many sky-viewing chambers designed by the American artist James Turrell, then lighting and illumination also play key roles in the interior choreography of the architecture. At the Supreme Court, a great ceremonial staircase cascades and tapers up to a window that offers a panoramic view to the Old City of Jerusalem. We next find ourselves beneath a tall pyramid or tent, a symbolic gateway to the law library, and, looking up, see its apex pierced by four small apertures. [10] Traversing the intersection of the building's axes, we enter a vast hall created between the concave stone wall that arcs through the entire project and an orthogonal wall of white plaster. This latter, blade-like surface is scalloped into a dozen semi-cylindrical apses, with low-level seating booths illuminated mysteriously from far above. These are the most attenuated geometries in Karmi-Melamede's lexicon, vertically extruded shafts that morph above to admit only a blush of north light. [11] The circulation route has ascended and looped before terminating in this long, high pool of light. We are here at one of the most sacred places in this secular temple, a cool public antechamber before the five individual courtrooms, each a little temple in itself.

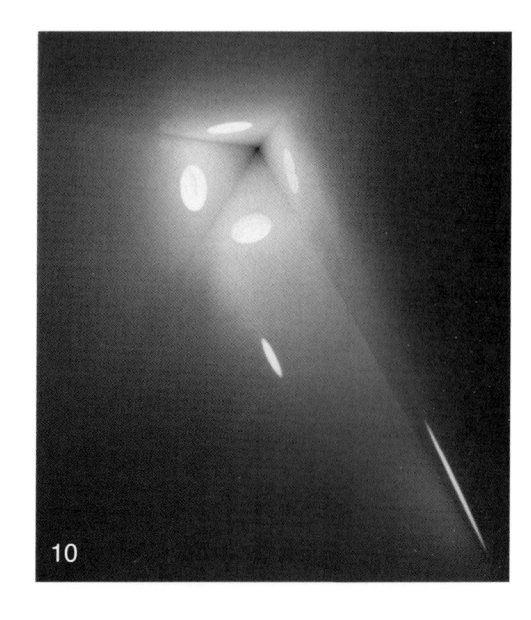

At the Open University, the courtyard sequence is external. Pedestrians arrive on transverse garden paths and funnel into a longitudinal colonnade with floors that rise or fall with the topography. The slanted exterior walls are cut into by rectangular openings to produce a lively staccato pattern of light and protective shade. [12] We proceed past some elegant, freestanding pavilions to a primary courtyard, angled in plan. This is the origin or landscape. [13] Internal partitions are tilted – splay in section – so that the sequence of passages is illuminated indirectly from above.

This prioritization of circulation, and the provision of multiple options for pedestrians, reflects Karmi-Melamede's concern for ground, the human experience, and the importance of exploration. Her work seeks to engage the public and the users of her buildings through what we might term realistic scenography.

At the Open University, the freestanding pavilions, housing a visitor centre and a luminous library, seem to combine two primary tropes in Israeli architecture: the historic solidity of Jerusalem and the more fluid openness of Bauhaus-inspired Tel Aviv, an Israel moulded not only by the architecture of Karmi-Melamede and her brother but, in earlier decades, by that of their father, Dov. Architecture is always somehow both bureaucratic and deeply personal, both a global and a local matter – it draws on images, procedures, materials and technology from across the world while simultaneously existing in a particular place, being constructed by particular people at a particular time.

The work of Ada Karmi-Melamede, demonstrated through these three very different projects, uses available knowledge and resources without abusing place. Her buildings fortify place, learning from and intensifying the character of urban, suburban and rural landscapes.

These places are ultimately at the service of a country's citizenry. For this foreign observer, memories of Israel, of this particular Israel, include young soldiers of Ethiopian descent visiting the Supreme Court, spirited technocrats occupying the Open University, and both post-punk teenagers and families in more traditional garments enjoying day trips to Ramat Hanadiv. Karmi-Melamede's approach to architecture facilitates and interweaves its civic function, its ability to gather people together in a collegial and inspirational way. Her fabrication and re-presentation of site, ground and place offer a prospect of serious work combined with the natural pleasures of life.

omphalos of the scheme. We are still outside. Entering the interior via the colonnade, we are embraced by a giant curving wall, as at the Supreme Court, and turn round to descend deep into the ground.

Down there, the internal street passes a double-storey bookshop with a delicate interior mezzanine (the balustrade in the architect's customary green/grey) and a billowing façade cut by horizontal ribbon fenestration – a subtle homage to the German organic architect Hans Scharoun. The subterranean galleria extends between the great bow of the curving concrete wall, pierced by its trio of skylights, and an orthogonal colonnade that carries down the rectilinear geometry and massing of the square patio upstairs. If the concrete, with its judicious incisions and teasing partial views, suggests an affinity with the work of contemporary Japanese master Tadao Ando, this re-presentation below grade of block-like, geometric forms is again suggestive of ruins and wall fragments. The earthwork has evolved into an inhabited spiral.

**Architecture for Exploration**

At Ramat Hanadiv, the Visitors Centre is designed to intensify rather than block the visitors' experience of the precious

*Raymund Ryan*

# The Visitors Centre – Ramat Hanadiv
Ada Karmi-Melamede Architects
Miller-Blum Landscape Architects

General view of the berm from the entrance

At the southern end of Mount Carmel near Zikhron Ya'akov, lies Ramat Hanadiv, a living memorial to Baron Edmond de Rothschild, comprised of a Nature Park and Memorial Gardens that are meticulously designed to allow for cultivated areas, natural spaces, foreign plants as well as local Israeli-Mediterranean ones. Each year, these parks welcome some 400,000 visitors, including many schoolchildren, who are guided through the Nature Park, the Memorial Gardens, and the history of the Rothschild family.

The Visitors Pavilion that we designed is largely hidden under a landscaped berm, which is planted with both wild and cultivated vegetation. The berm building acts as a divider between the incoming vehicular traffic and the pedestrian entrance to the Memorial Gardens. Richly planted with trees and shrubs, the Pavilion has a gentle curvilinear form whose focal point is well inside the Memorial Gardens. Its convex southern side establishes the boundary of the parking area and the natural park that lies beyond it; its concave northern side is covered with the cultivated plants characteristic of the Memorial Gardens that it embraces. The intermediate space between the Pavilion and the Memorial Gardens entrance gate forms an expansive, open-air foyer. This space widens at its center and narrows at both ends, gently focusing attention to the Gardens' entrance. Three pathways intersect the Pavilion and reveal its depth and structure. They allow the public to cross from the parking area to the open foyer and to enter the various functions housed in the Pavilion. The central pathway, which is also the widest, leads to the major axis of the Memorial Gardens, which itself leads to the crypt of Baron and Baroness de Rothschild.

The Pavilion's envelope is formed by two concrete curving surfaces that lean against each other, without touching. Within this dynamic space, all the functions of the Pavilion are located and nurtured by indirect light from above. The Pavilion's plan is simple – a central, curved public spine runs through the entire length of the building, parallel to the curved exterior walls. As one walks along the spine, it expands and narrows, ascends and descends, with its extremities remaining always beyond view. With a stone clad service tunnel on one side and tall plastered walls on the other that house all public functions, the spine is suffused with indirect, natural light that issues from the gap between the berm's inclined surfaces. This light causes the interior to glow softly and irregularly. The light wanders, reflects and surprises all day long. Along the spine's length, spaces

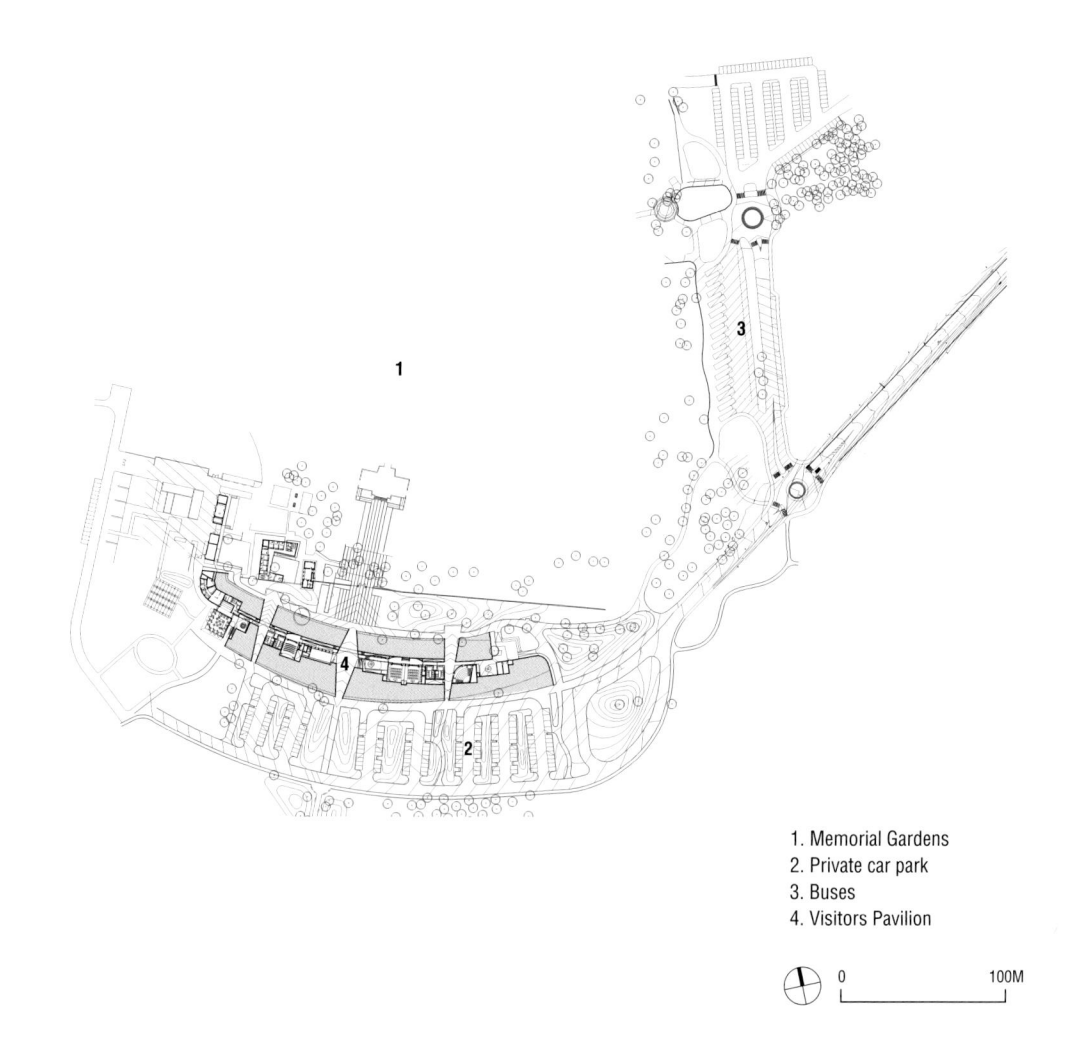

1. Memorial Gardens
2. Private car park
3. Buses
4. Visitors Pavilion

0    100M

Visitors Pavilion (hidden under a landscaped berm)

Master Plan
1. Parking
2. Pathways
3. Entrance to the
   Memorial Gardens
4. Administrative offices
5. Visitors Pavilion
6. Support facilities

0  50M

Aerial view of the site

of various sizes house classrooms and auditoriums, an exhibition hall, a cafeteria, and a gift shop. The variable elements of these consistently curved spaces are the height, light, and the focal point of each one. On occasion, the spine opens up into interior courtyards. Along its route, it is also intersected by the three main pathways leading from the parking area to the Gardens. At either end of the Pavilion, the spine terminates with multipurpose and larger public spaces that open up to the sky and offer views to the east and to the west.

Much effort was invested in both the planning and construction of the building in order to reduce its environmental impact. Of particular note, a geothermal air-conditioning system was installed, which exchanges the heat of the building with low ground temperatures instead of transferring it to the outside air – a system that mitigates greenhouse gas emissions. In a similar way, measures were taken to reduce overall energy consumption through smart design, choice of materials and appropriate landscaping. The building is mostly subterranean and is sealed using multiple layers of insulation and a vapour barrier. Semi-dry stone construction was used with an air space between the stone and the concrete, improving insulation and conserving energy costs.

16

1. Entrance
2. Auditorium
3. Classroom
4. Inner courtyard
5. Exhibition space and gift shop
6. Lecture hall
7. Inner courtyard
8. Coffee shop
9. Inner passage spine
10. Administrative offices
11. Pedestrian pathways

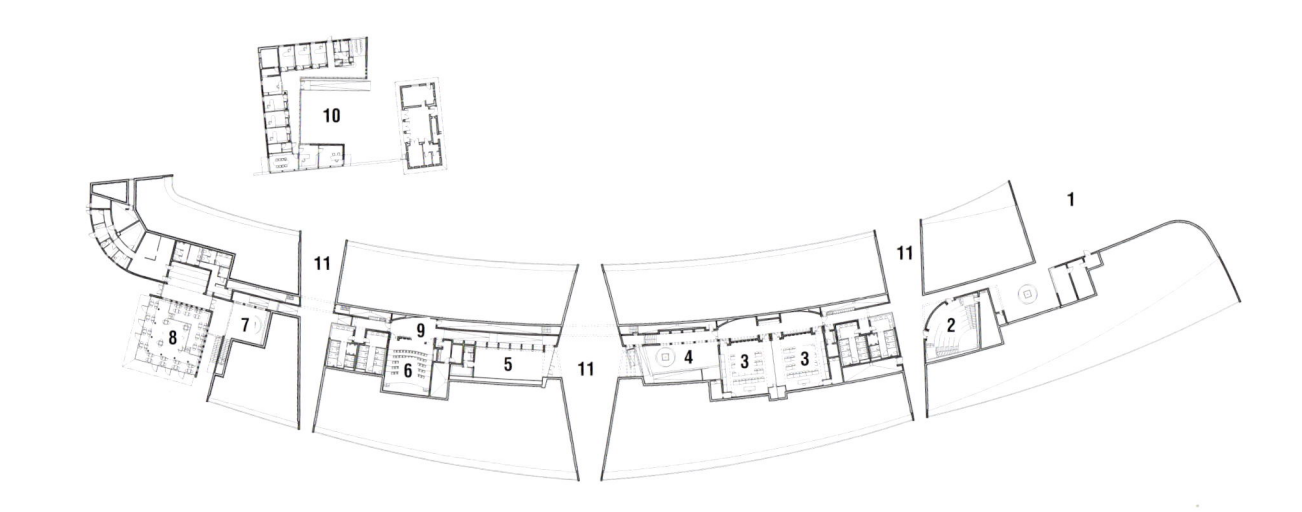

Bird's-eye view of the Gardens and the town of Zikhron Ya'akov

A wastewater purification facility was created, which produces water irrigation for the grounds. Most materials were quarried at the site and all building waste was collected there. Remnants of stone cladding, flooring, gravel, sand, ceramics, etc. were crushed and used on site to cover the berm planting bed. All wood forms used during construction were shredded and used as ground cover in the landscaping, thereby decreasing irrigation needs. The Visitors Centre opened to the public in 2008 and was one of the first buildings in Israel to comply with Israel's Code 5281 – the standard for sustainable buildings with reduced environmental impact – with Distinction. The building was subsequently granted LEED certification, the current international standard for green construction.

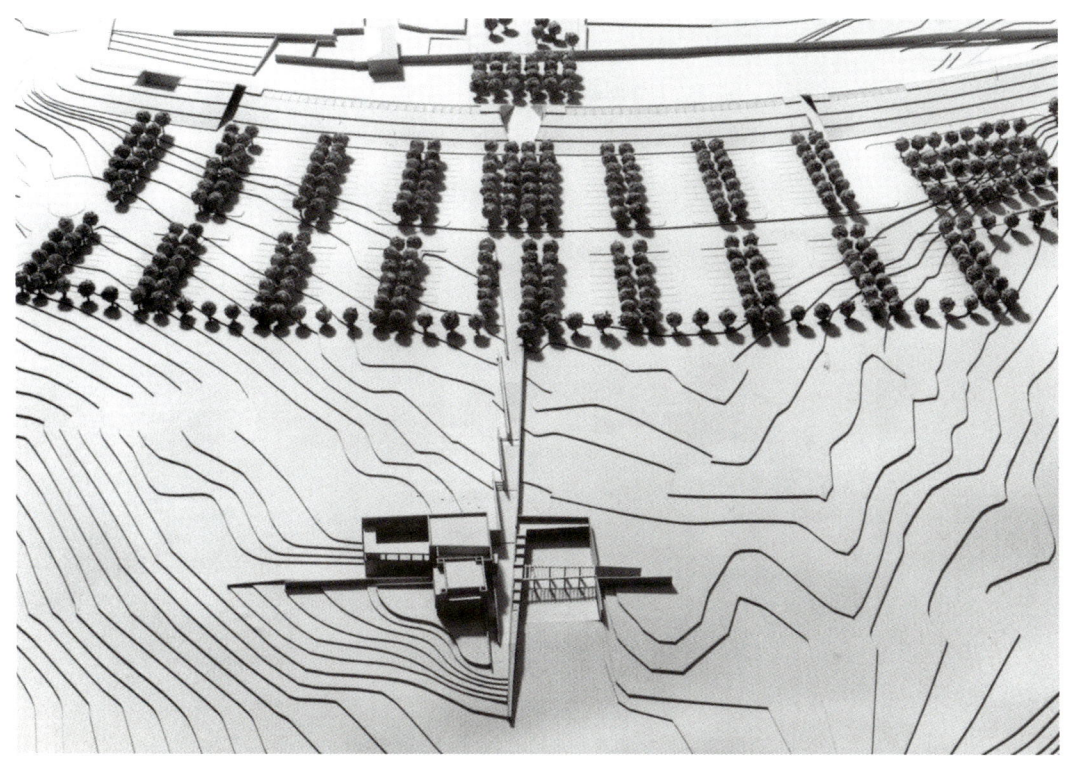

*Ada Karmi-Melamede and Guy Teomi*

Above left and right:
Model – light penetration

Left:
First design proposal

Inner courtyard

Entrance to the auditorium from the pathway

Section A

Section B

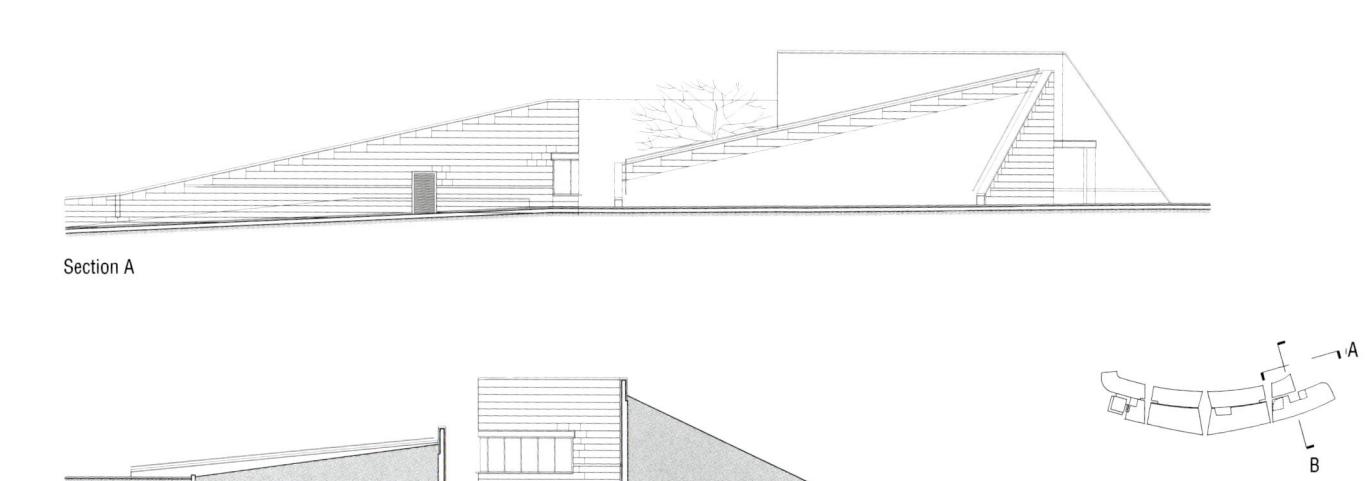

0    5M

0   5M

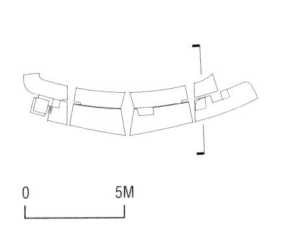

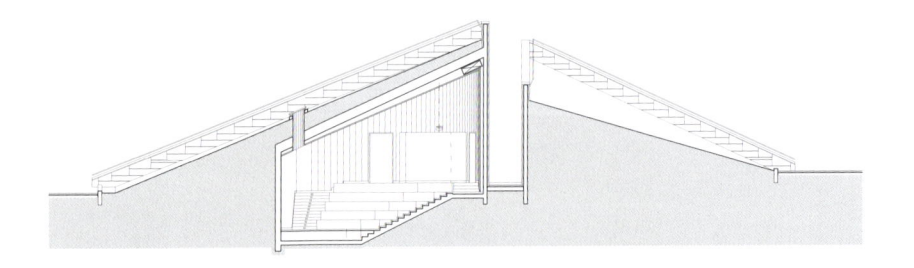

Left:
Auditorium

Right:
Pathway

22

Right above:
The concave northern side of the berm covered with cultivated plants

Right below:
The central pathway leading to the gate of the Memorial Gardens from the parking area

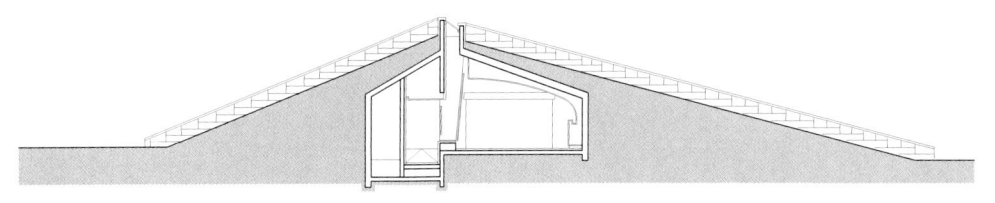

Section A

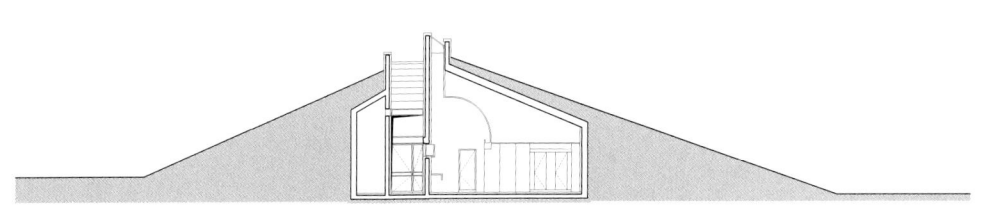

Section B

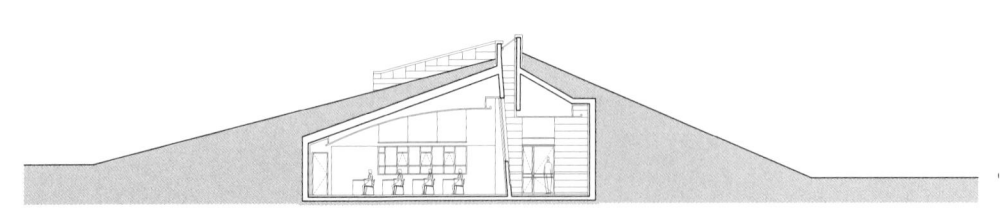

Section C

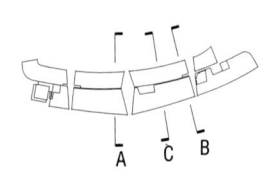

A  C  B

0    5M

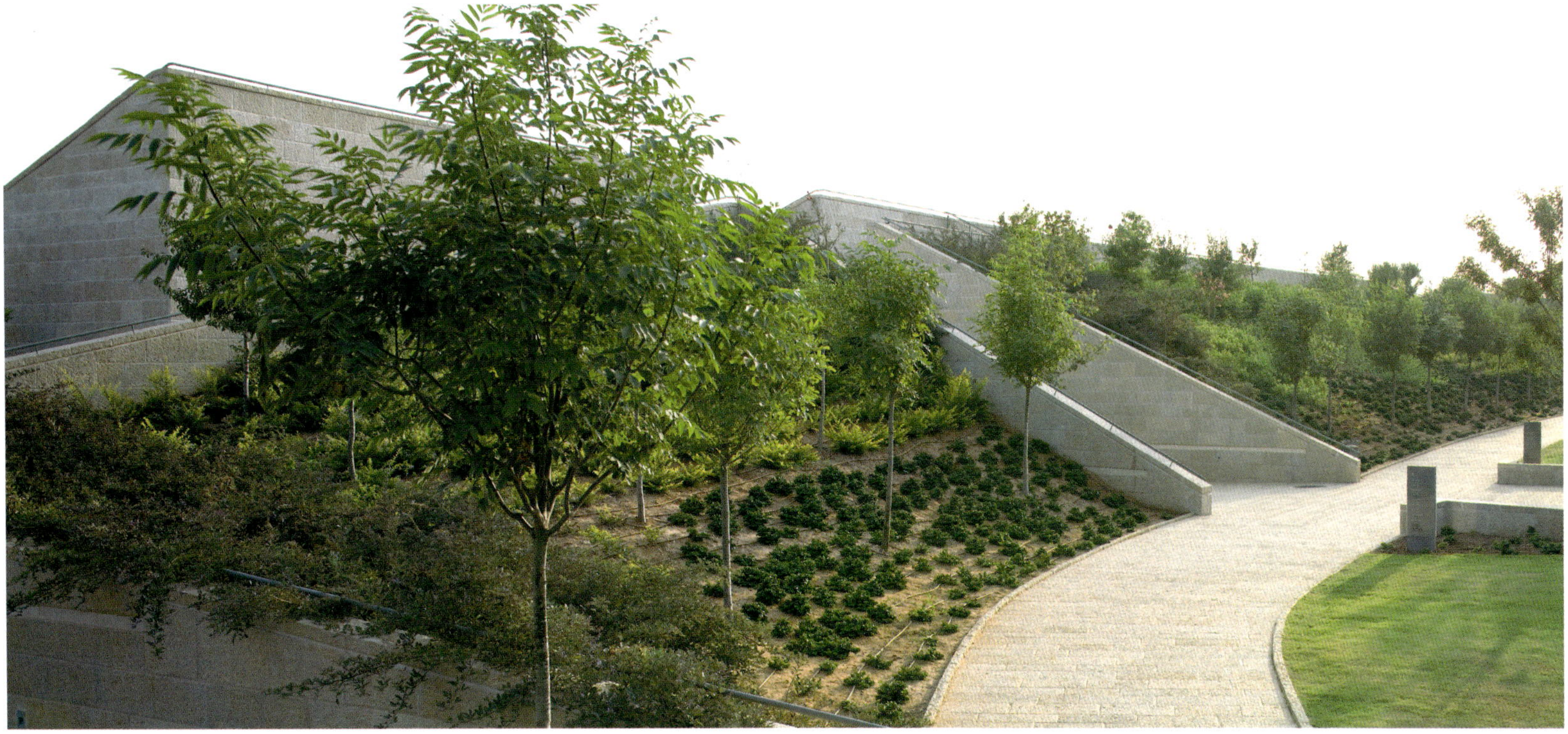

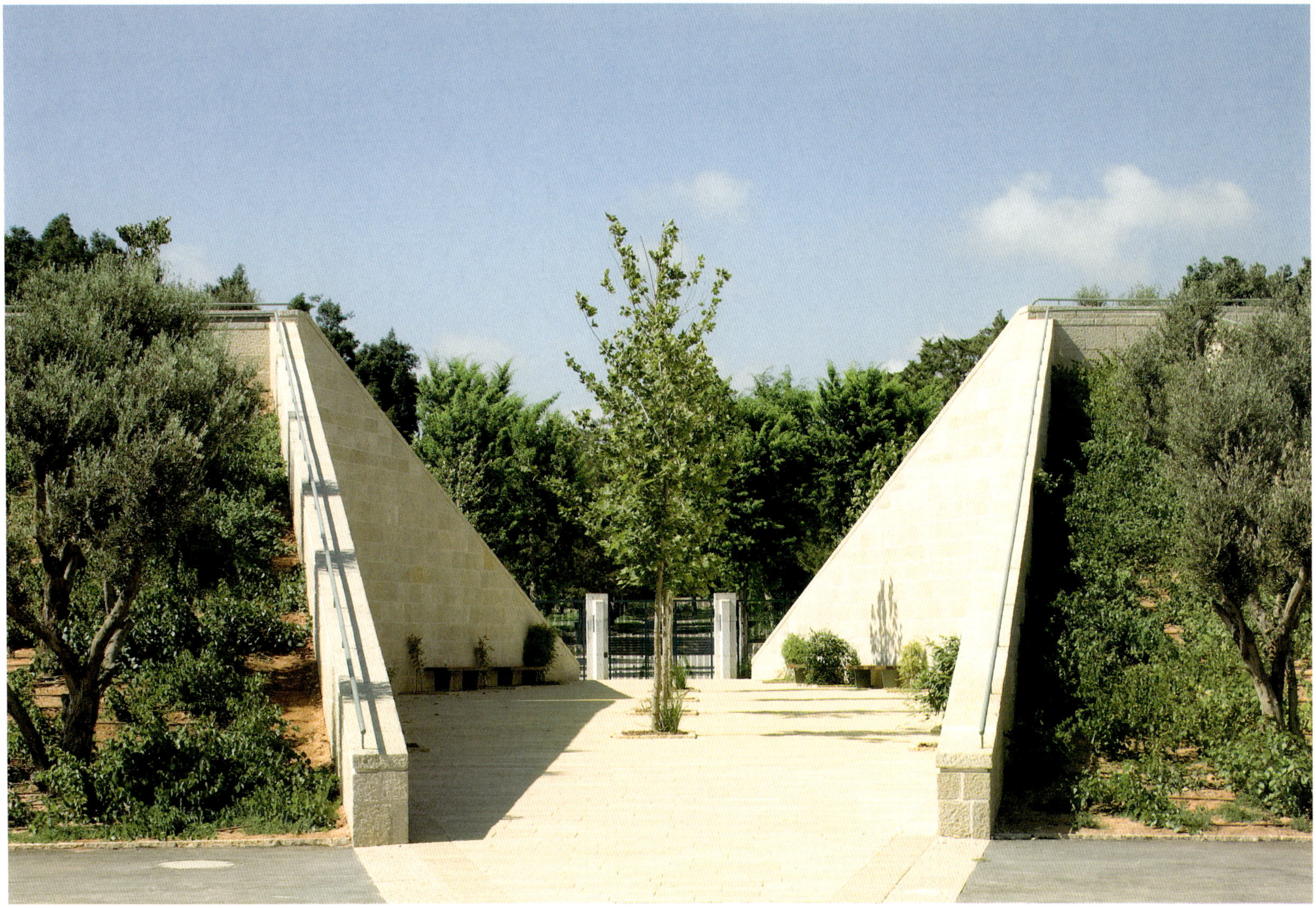

Left:
The inner 'spine' passing along the exhibition area.

Right:
A detail of the indirect light which runs through the entire length of the spine.

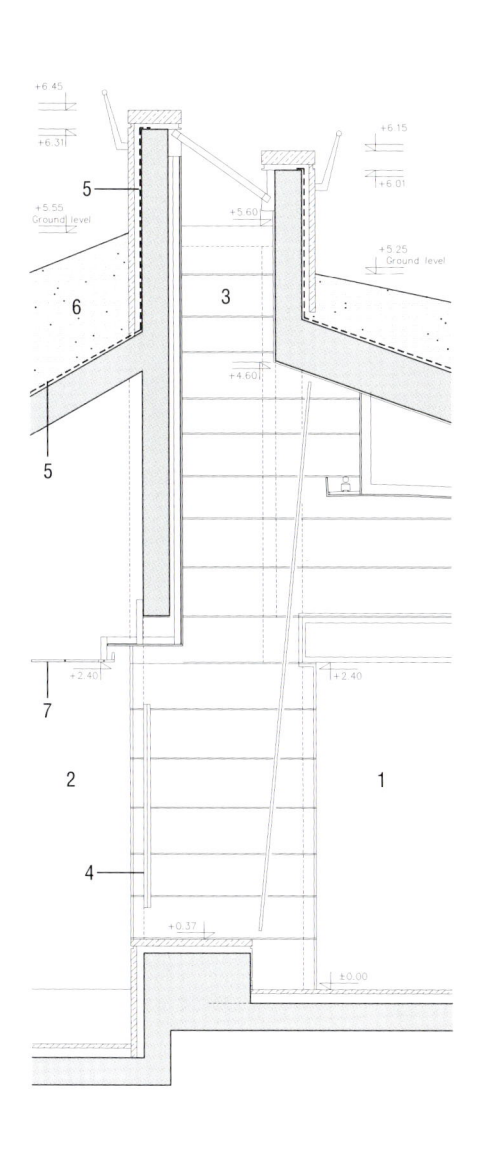

1. Exhibition gallery
2. Internal spine
3. Light shaft
4. Glass partition
5. Insulation vapour barrier
6. Soil
7. Hung wooden ceiling

0    1M

The 'spine' leading to the classroom and the inner courtyard

Lecture hall

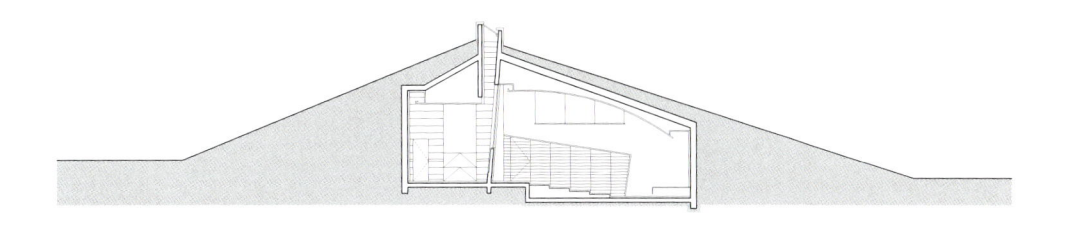

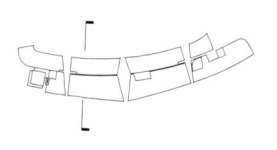

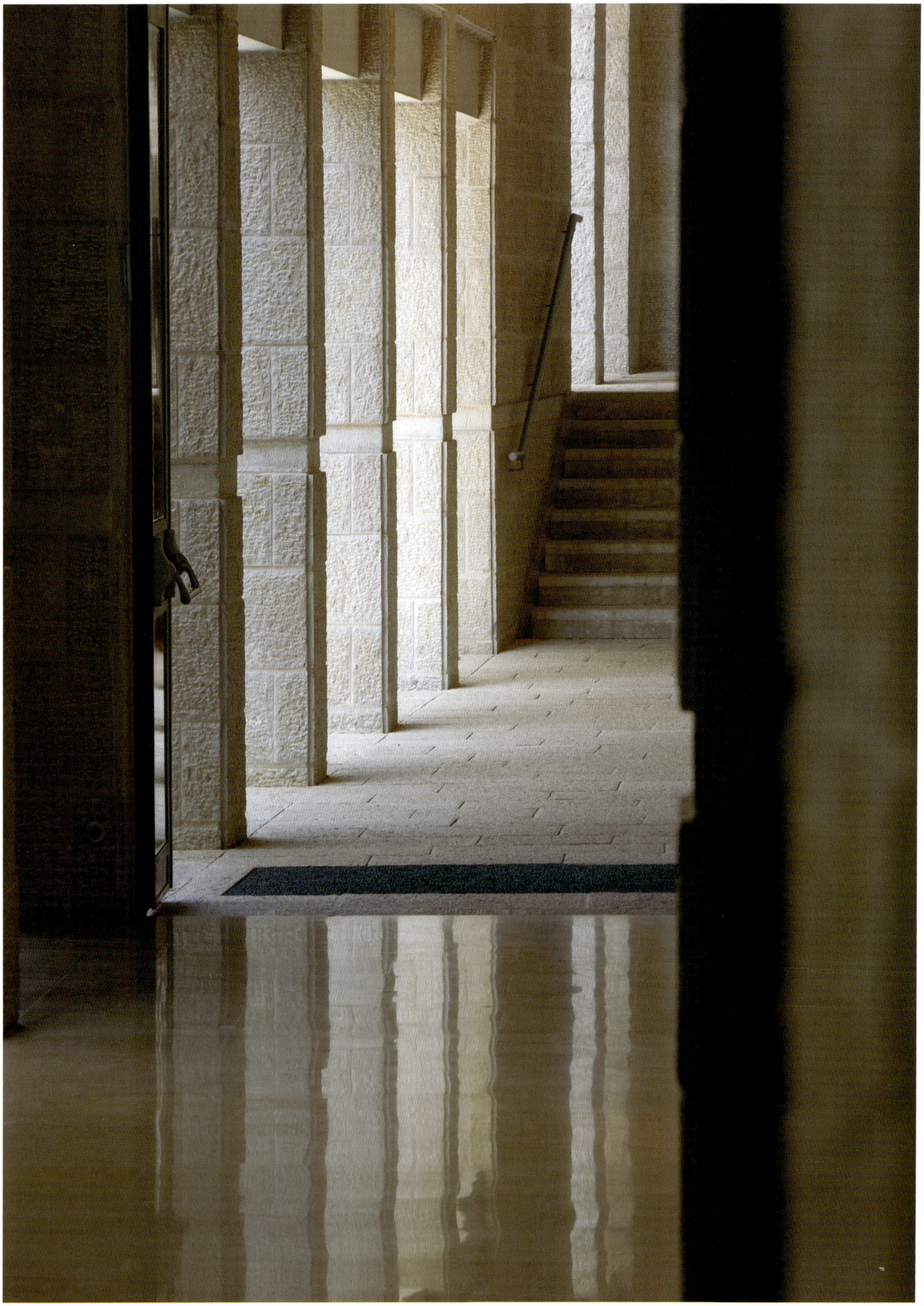

Left:
The 'spine' moving between inside and outside

Right:
Detail: indirect light bouncing off the structural columns

Section A

Section B

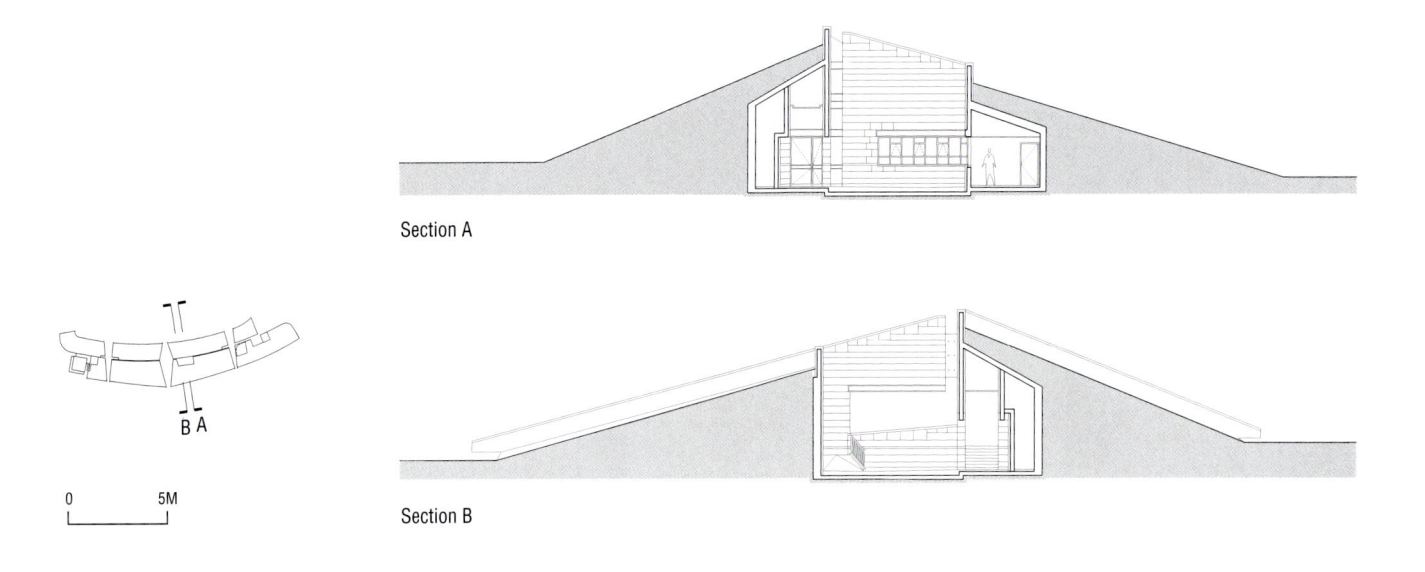

0  5M

Inner courtyard

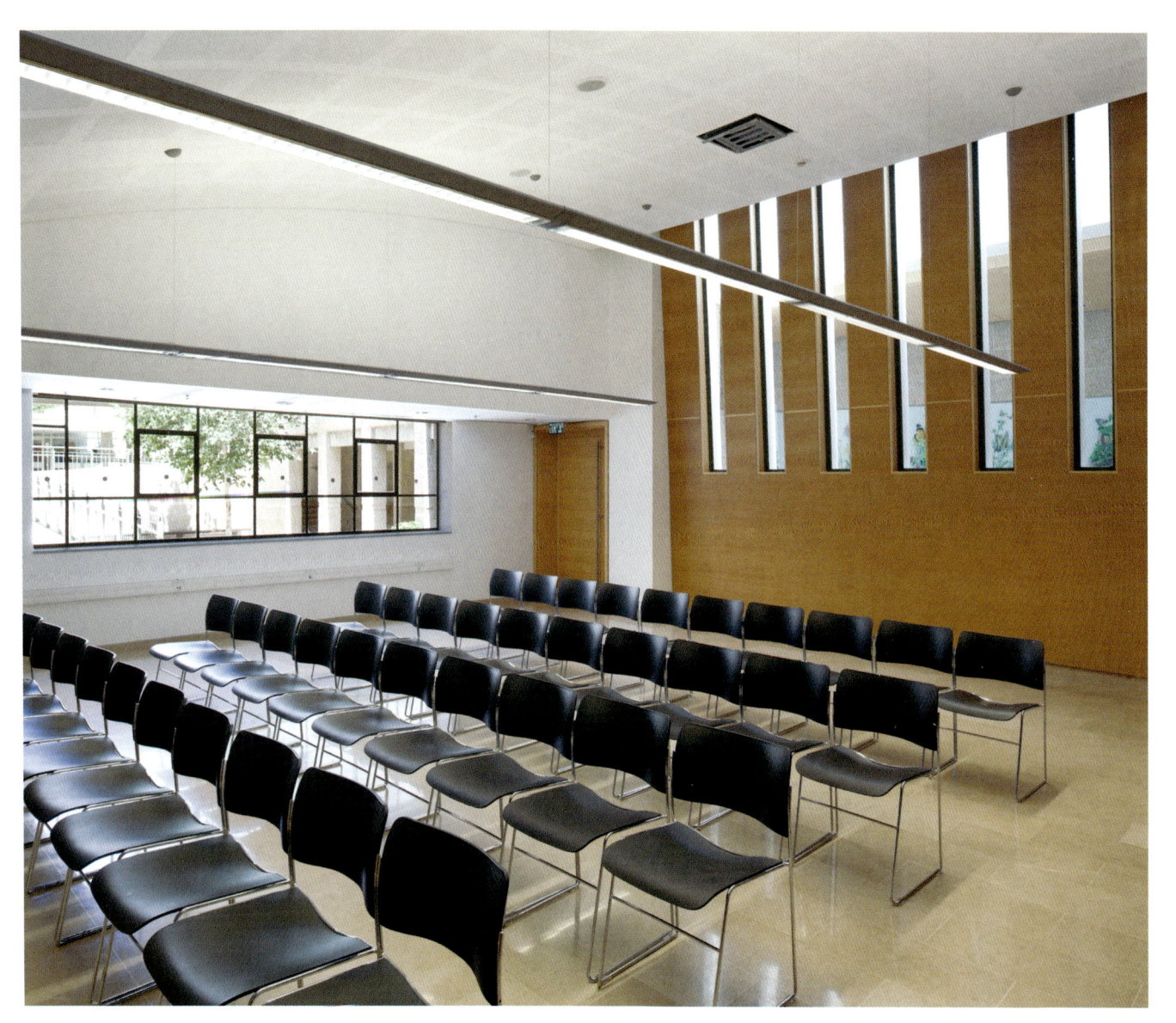

Classroom

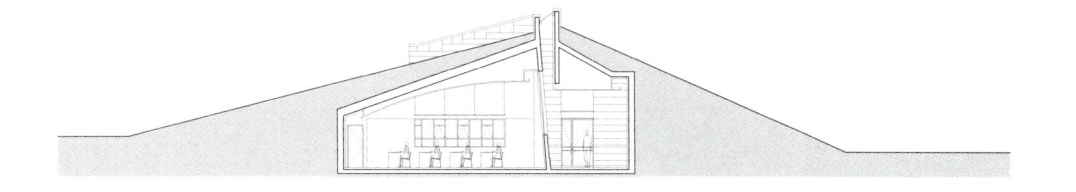

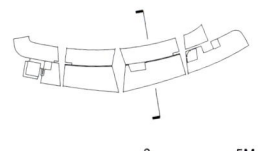

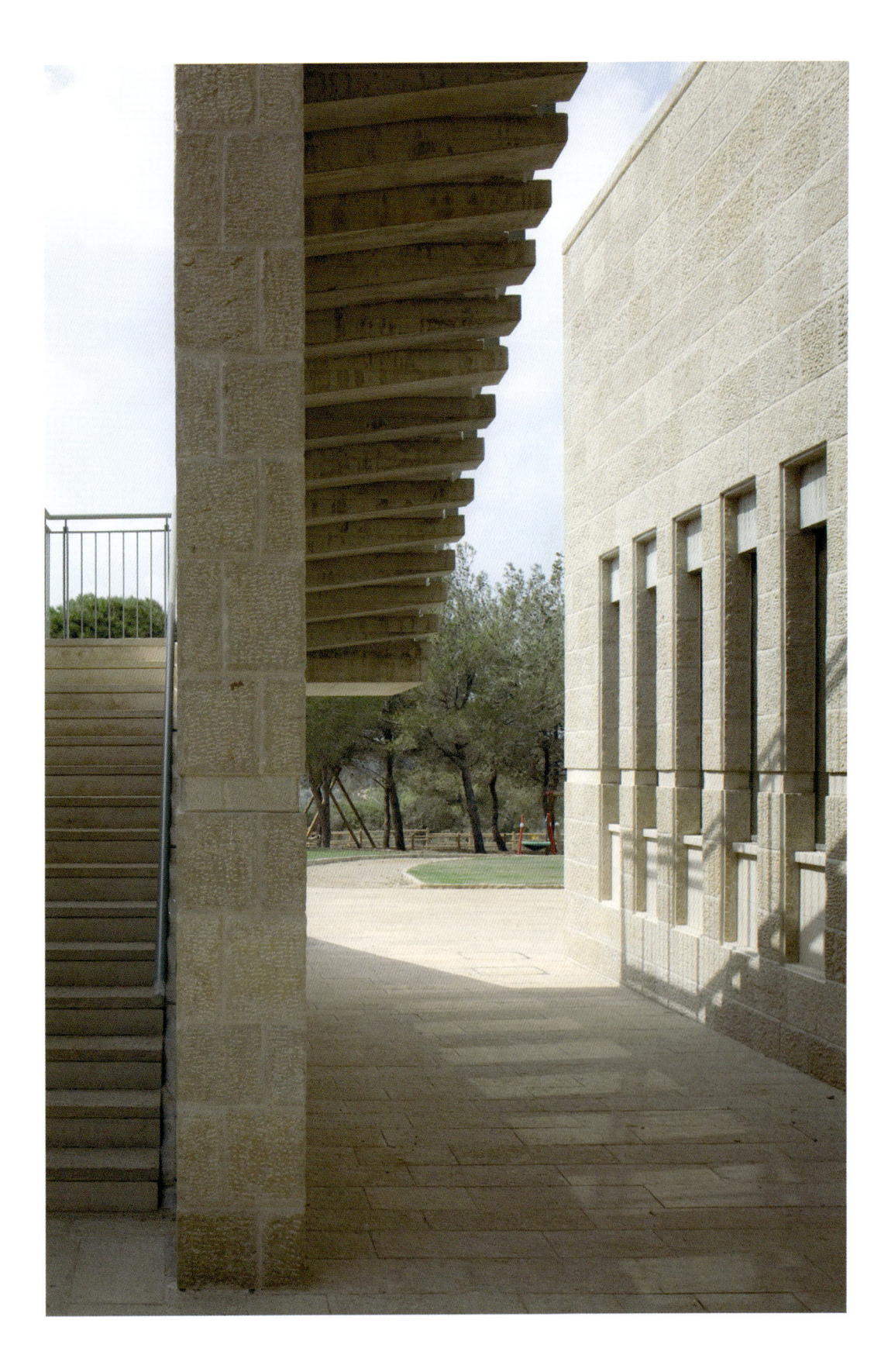

Left:
Stair leading to
viewing platform above

Right:
The inner courtyard adjacent
to the coffee shop

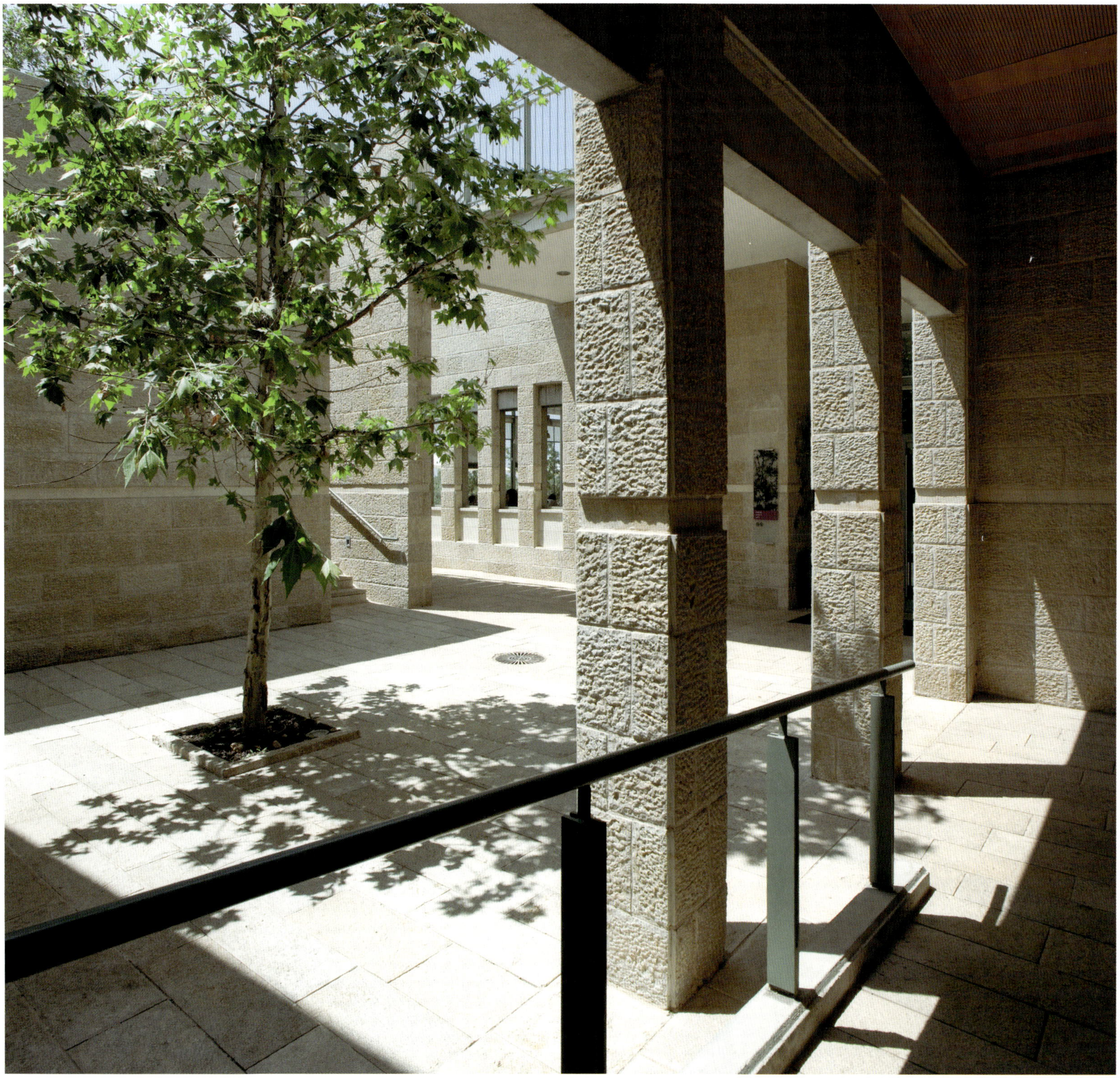

Coffee shop

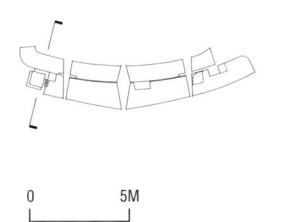

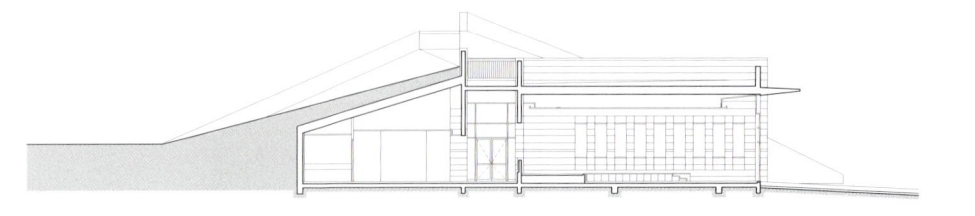

0  5M

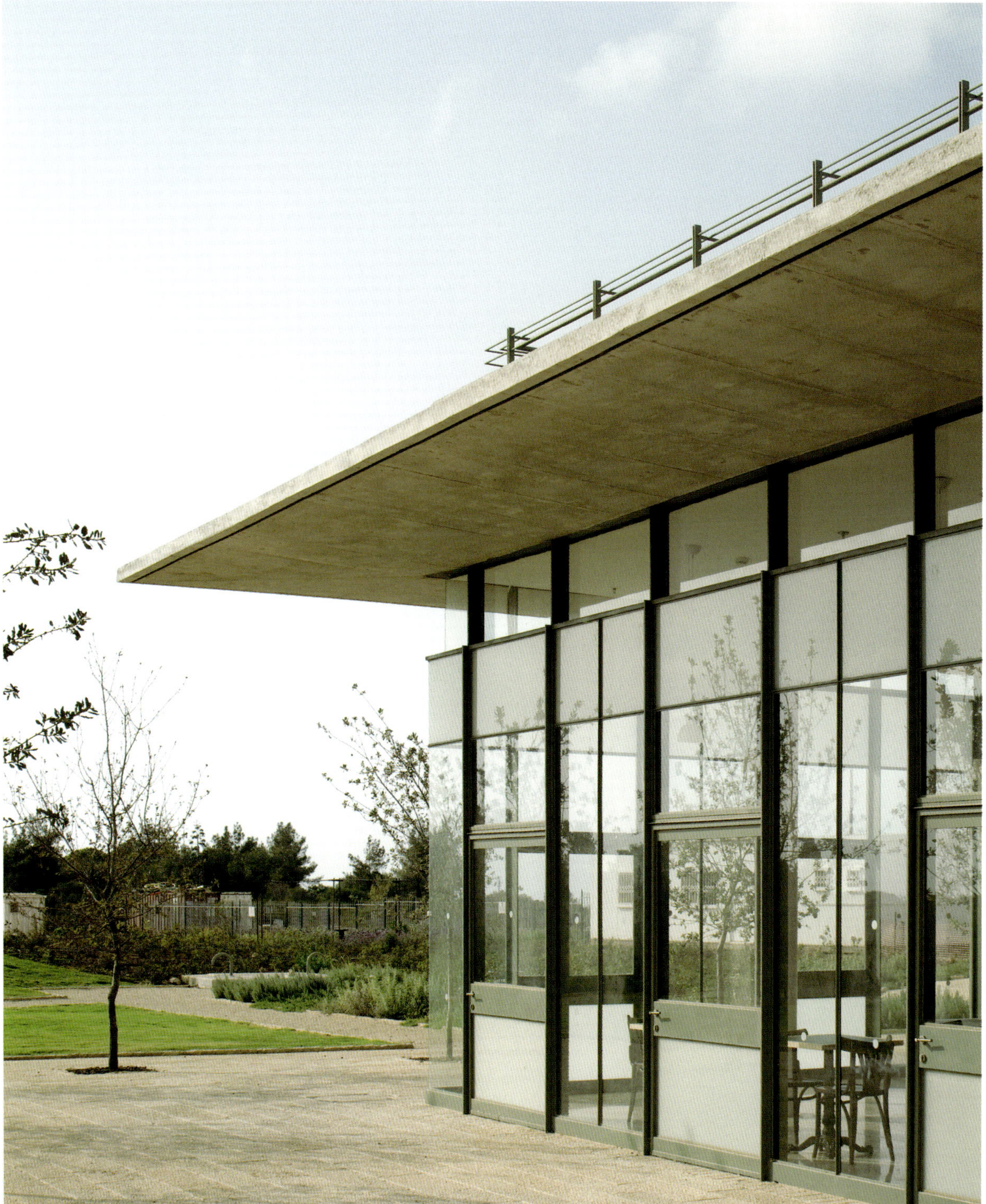

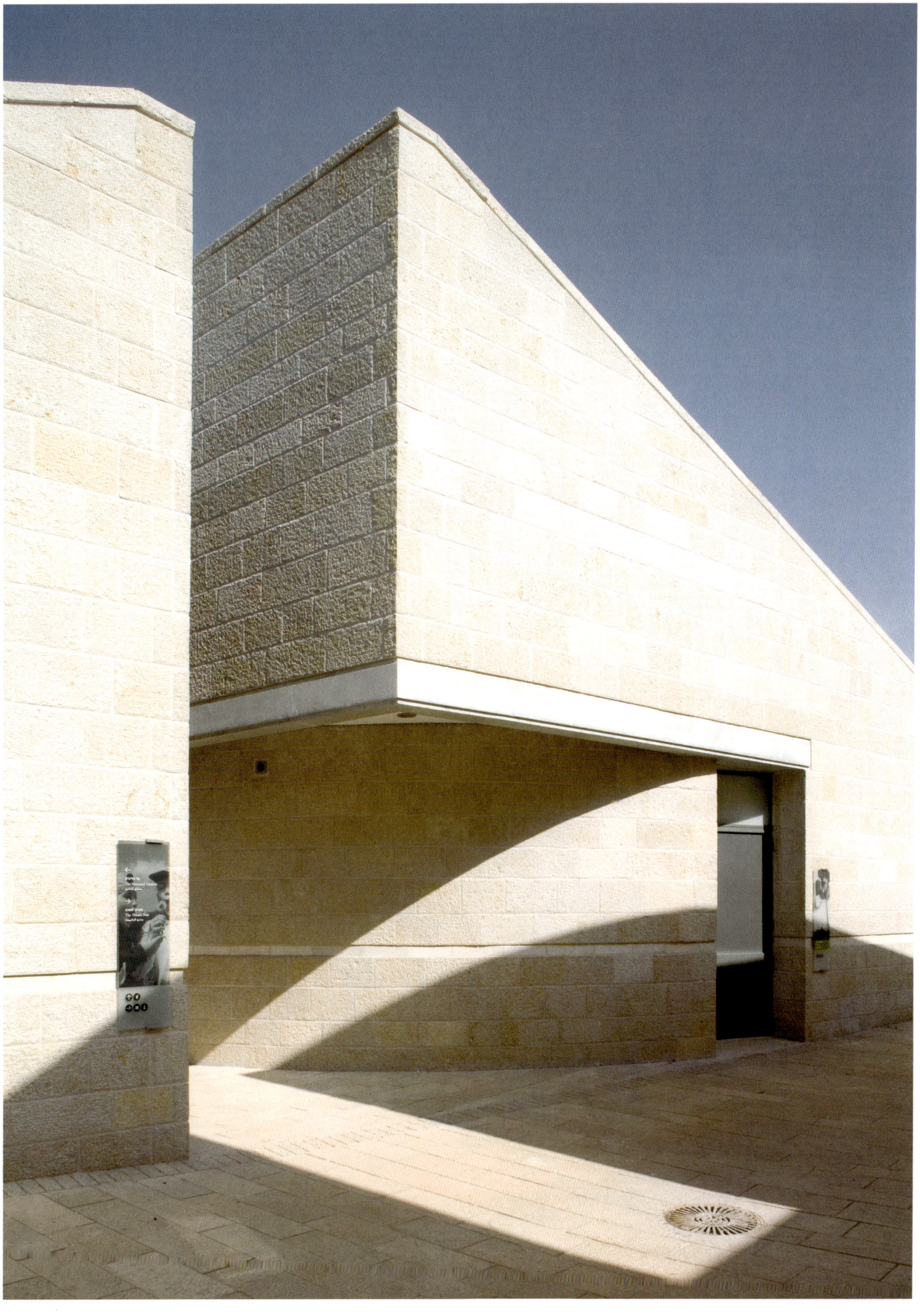

Left:
Entrance to the auditorium
from the public pathway

Right:
Public W.C.

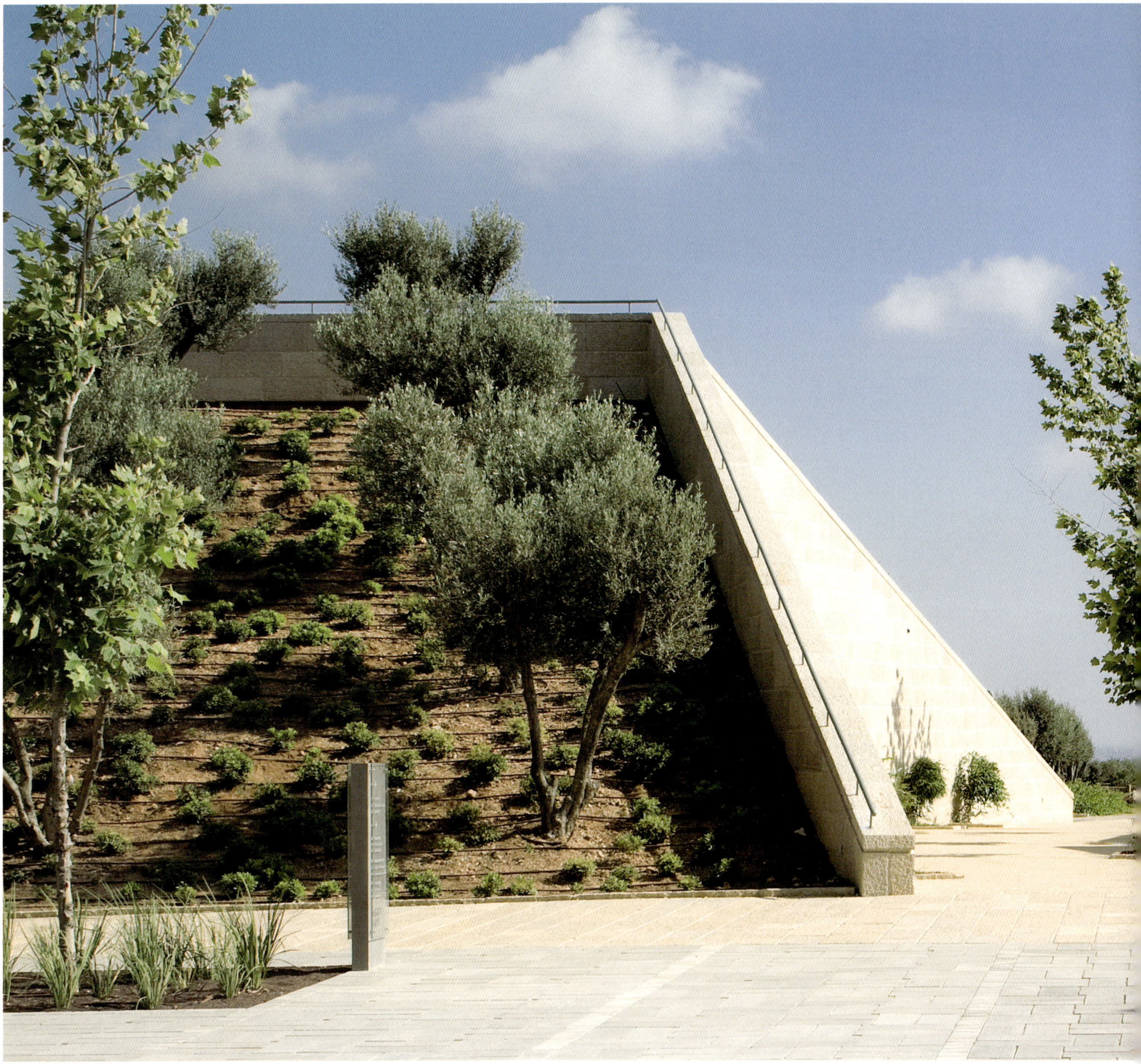

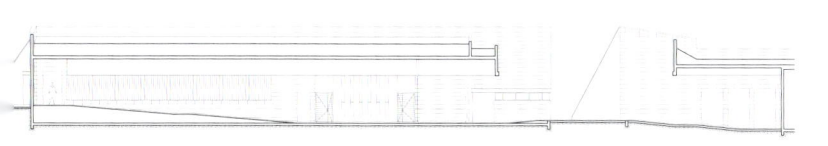

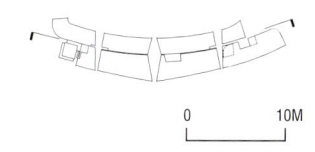

Central pathway leading from the Memorial Gardens to the parking area and the natural reserve

0  10M

# The Open University – Ra'anana

Ada Karmi-Melamede Architects
Dan Tzur Landscape Architects

View from the sunken garden

# The Open University – Ra'anana

The Open University of Israel (OUI) is the largest university in the country and caters almost exclusively to distance learning. Instructional materials, publications, online broadcasts, lectures, and student services exist and are directed at a student body whose presence and personality is almost entirely absent from the campus. Students visit campus in order to register for classes, to receive guidance on occasion, and to complete work or matriculate. For them, the campus is a place of information, not of learning. Apart from a handful of meetings that they will have there, they are directed to virtual learning sites that are accessed from anywhere and everywhere.

OUI was founded in the early 1970s and was modelled after the UK's Open University. Its built past was a humble one in northern Tel Aviv, which offered nothing remarkable in terms of its architectural memory that could be mined for the new site. Its philosophical underpinnings – its emphasis on openness, academic excellence and a community of learning – did, however, suggest a university heritage of former times. Rather than a transient student population, OUI caters to a more permanent population of academics, administrators and researchers. It houses typical functions of a university, such as lecture rooms, library and administration, but it requires a great number of faculty offices for the preparation of the learning material and many studios for recording and broadcasting.

The campus site is located in the heart of the Sharon region, on the outskirts of the city of Ra'anana and its border with Kfar Saba. The parcel of land stretches between two utterly dissimilar roads. One is a regional highway running along the eastern edge of the site and the other is a typical Ra'anana neighborhood tree-lined street along the western side. Taking into consideration the campus's position of being wedged between two very distinct situations – the regional and the municipal – the design for the campus is one that develops in layers. This layered quality proceeds from the massive and national scale of the eastern façade, which responds to the fast rhythm of traffic along its edge, to the smaller, more local scale of the western façade, which relates to the adjacent neighborhood. This hierarchy, from the national to the local, is present in every physical facet of the architectural composition – including density, volumetric layout, building, façades and materials.

Three narrow bands of buildings cross the campus site: the first band, which is the arterial edge, houses administration functions, technology and communications; the second band serves special functions, including the library, the synagogue, and a visitors centre; the third band, which is the neighborhood edge, holds the academic faculty, research

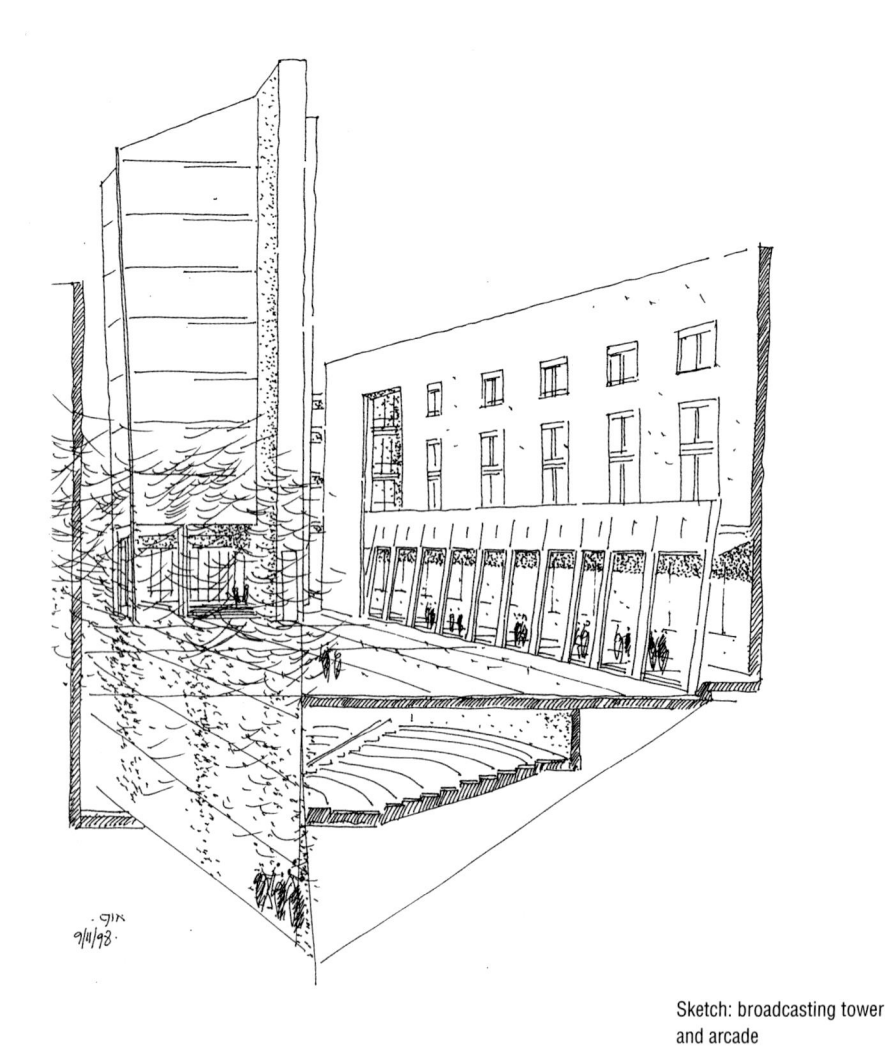

Sketch: broadcasting tower and arcade

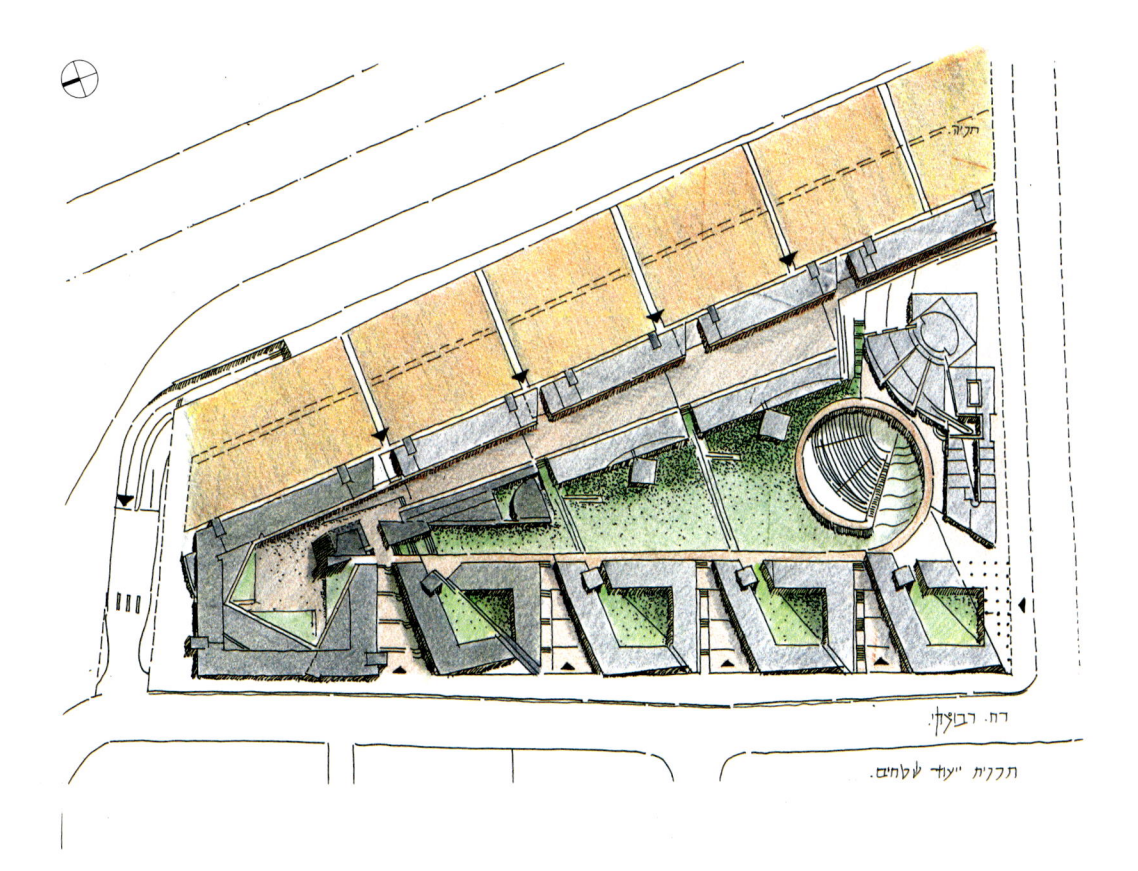

Master plan

groups and curriculum-planning teams. Between these bands of buildings are green belts that extend the entire length of the site from north to south. These form the pedestrian walkways of the campus and merge together at both ends of the campus into public-scaled outdoor spaces – a large courtyard at one end and an amphitheater at the other.

The campus fabric undulates with changing levels of the site and is layered both vertically and horizontally. The views into the large courtyard reveal its different facets. Standing at the lowest elevation, the courtyard appears floating and object-like; from its highest point, the courtyard appears fixed and rooted firmly into the ground; and from above, it appears both closed and open. These contradictions exist simultaneously, creating a dynamic space that is both familiar and surprising.

The courtyard is the hub and fulcrum of the institution and contains a dense concentration of functions that serve students, employees, and visitors. It is an urban space defined by its formal geometry of stone-covered walls, a concrete arcade and a defined structural

Master Plan and First Phase Development

1. The public plaza
2. Students and administration facilities
3. Faculty offices
4. Sunken garden
5. Parking
6. Regional road
7. Local street

Ada Karmi-Melamede, Architects

Sunken garden surrounded by a retaining wall

rhythm. Alternating light and shadows strengthen the rhythms of the structure, elongating and shortening perspectives, and changing the architectural experience within the arcade each and every hour.

The green band that leads away from it – the wadi, opens up gradually across the campus, and terminates in a large garden that houses the open air amphitheatre. This wadi 'celebrates' the freedom of green, open space.

The visitors centre is nestled at the intersection of the urban courtyard and the wadi. It offers a unique vantage point onto the gradual transformation of the campus from an urban landscape on one side to a green and pastoral one on the other. It is a dialogue between the inconstant and the constant; between the architectural tradition of the amphitheatre, familiar to us from ages long past, and the methods and tools of modern education that are in a constant state of flux. Despite its many diverse functions, and the complexity of the master plan, the campus maintains its singular mood through the spatial sequence and the nature of its materiality. All the buildings' public spaces on the ground level and below it are expressed in cast concrete, which lends them weight, authority and permanence. Stone walls delineate the more private spaces above – these are detailed, more personal and elegant.

Between the richness of materials – the stone, concrete, and plaster – the entire atmosphere of place changes with the fluctuations of light and shadow, shifting constantly between heavy and light, permanent and transient, static and dynamic.
The OUI's spatial sequence responds to a particular program, topography and climate. While only the first phases of the campus have been completed, the design of the master plan envisions a procession of public spaces that allows for an efficient and modular future expansion that will hopefully reaffirm and compliment the first phases.

The current buildings – exposed and concealed – that exist within the architectural composition of the campus are materially and spatially complex. They invite different interpretations depending on where they are experienced from, the behaviour of the light at any given moment, and where one is going. From the exterior, the forms are more static, massive, unambiguous, but here too, ever-changing light affects their presence and their weight. The multi-dimensional orchestration of the scheme and its inherent diversity between urban and garden environments have hopefully created a rich environment for social and academic interaction that has room to evolve long into the future amid a scenery that will only grow greener with the passage of time.

*Ada Karmi-Melamede*

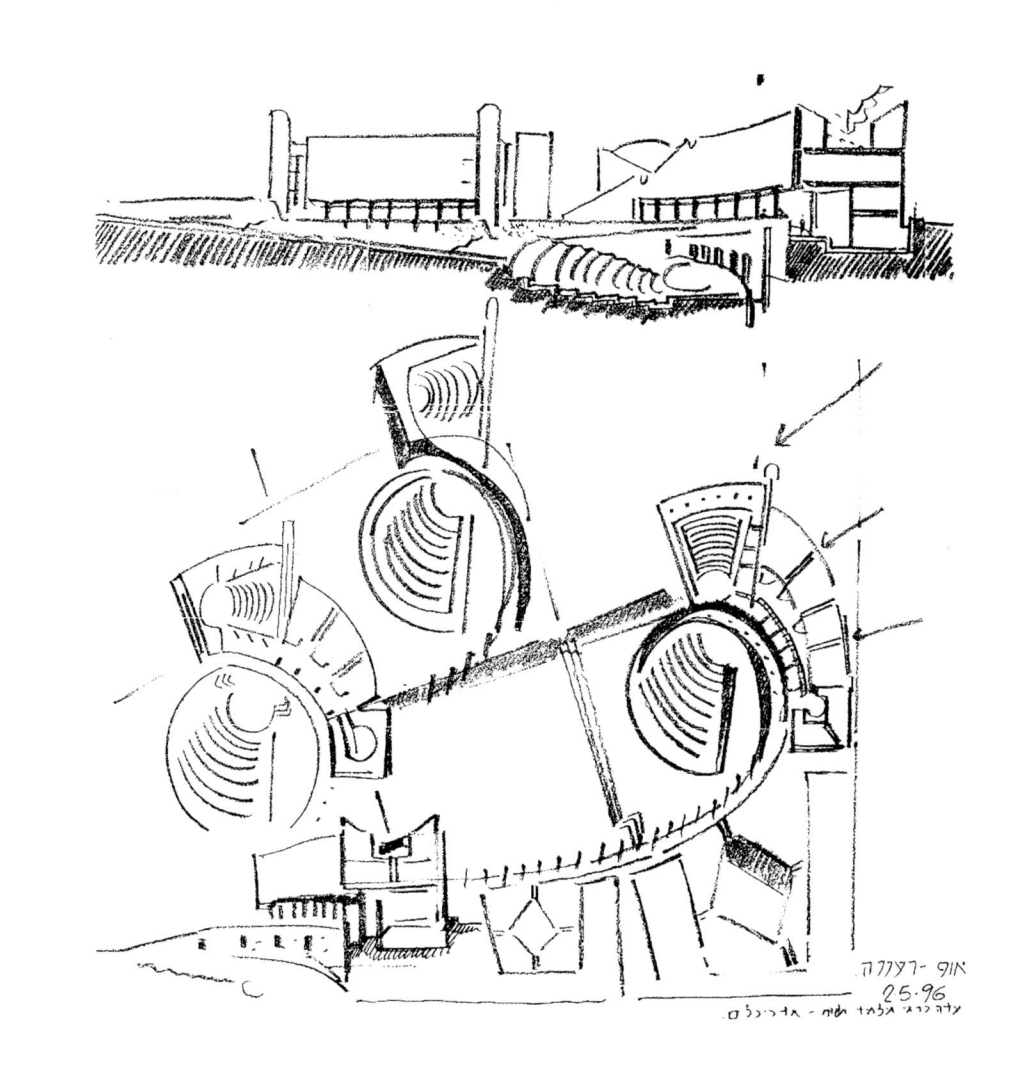

Sketch: theatre and amphitheatre located at the garden edge

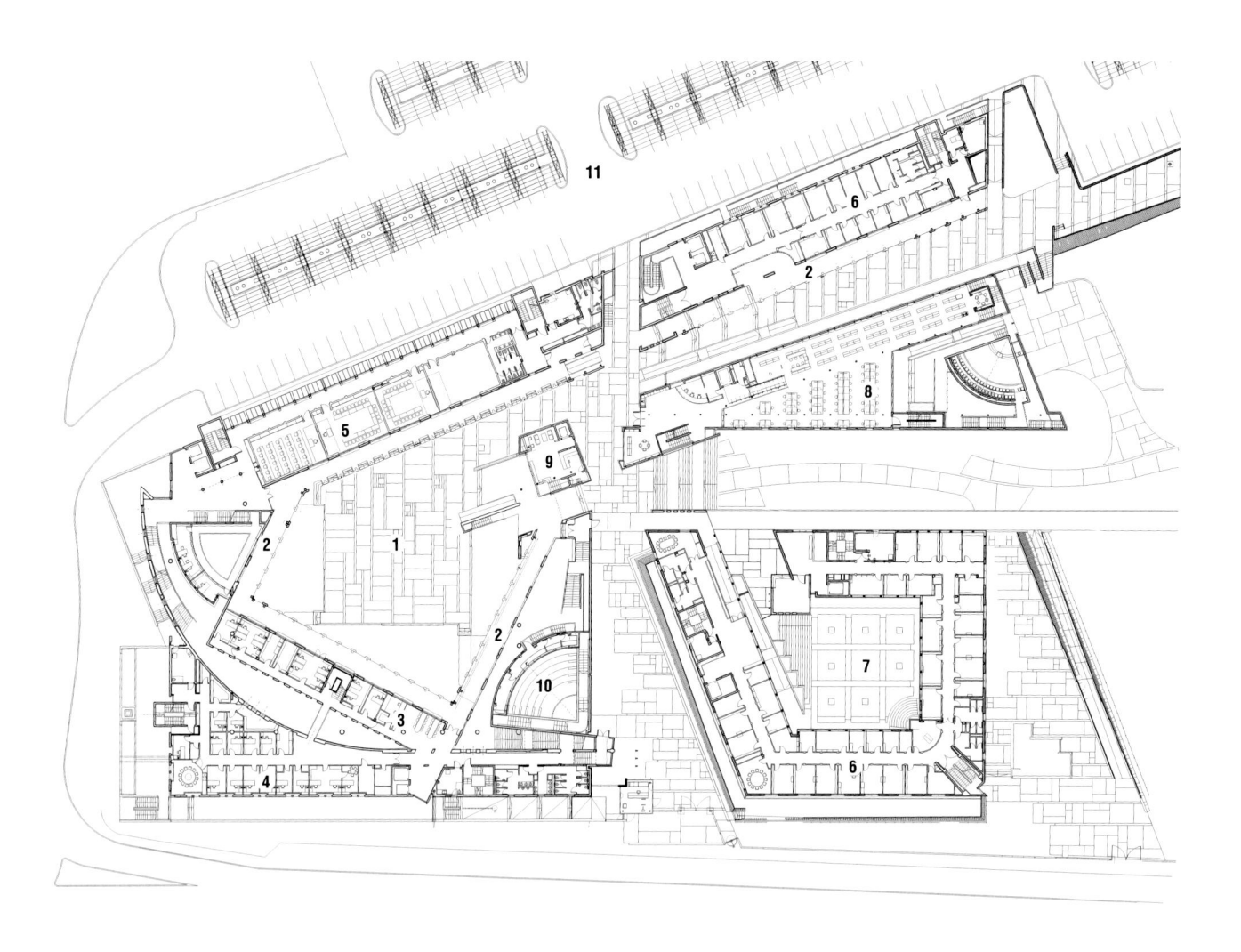

Entrance Level Plan

1. Public plaza
2. Arcade
3. Students facilities
4. Administration
5. Classrooms
6. Faculty offices
7. Sunken courtyard
8. Library
9. Visitors centre
10. Small auditorium
11. Parking

0   25 M

47

0    25 M

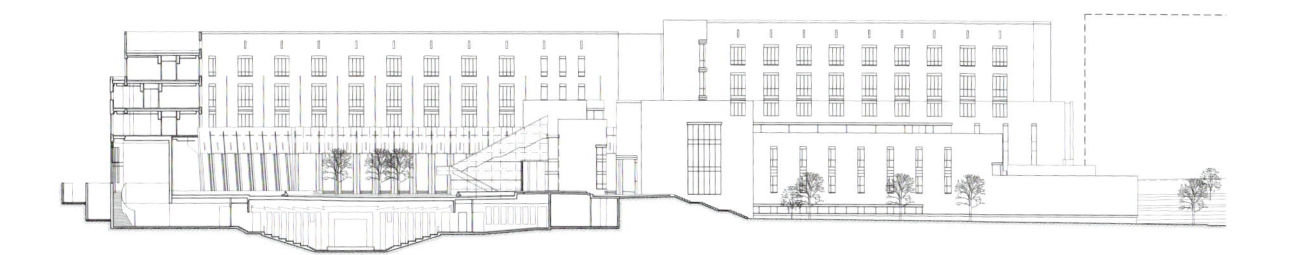

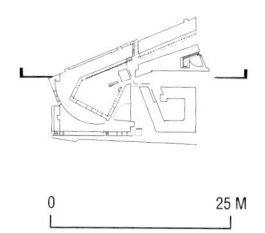

Below left:
View towards visitors centre

Below right:
Entrance from the
parking area

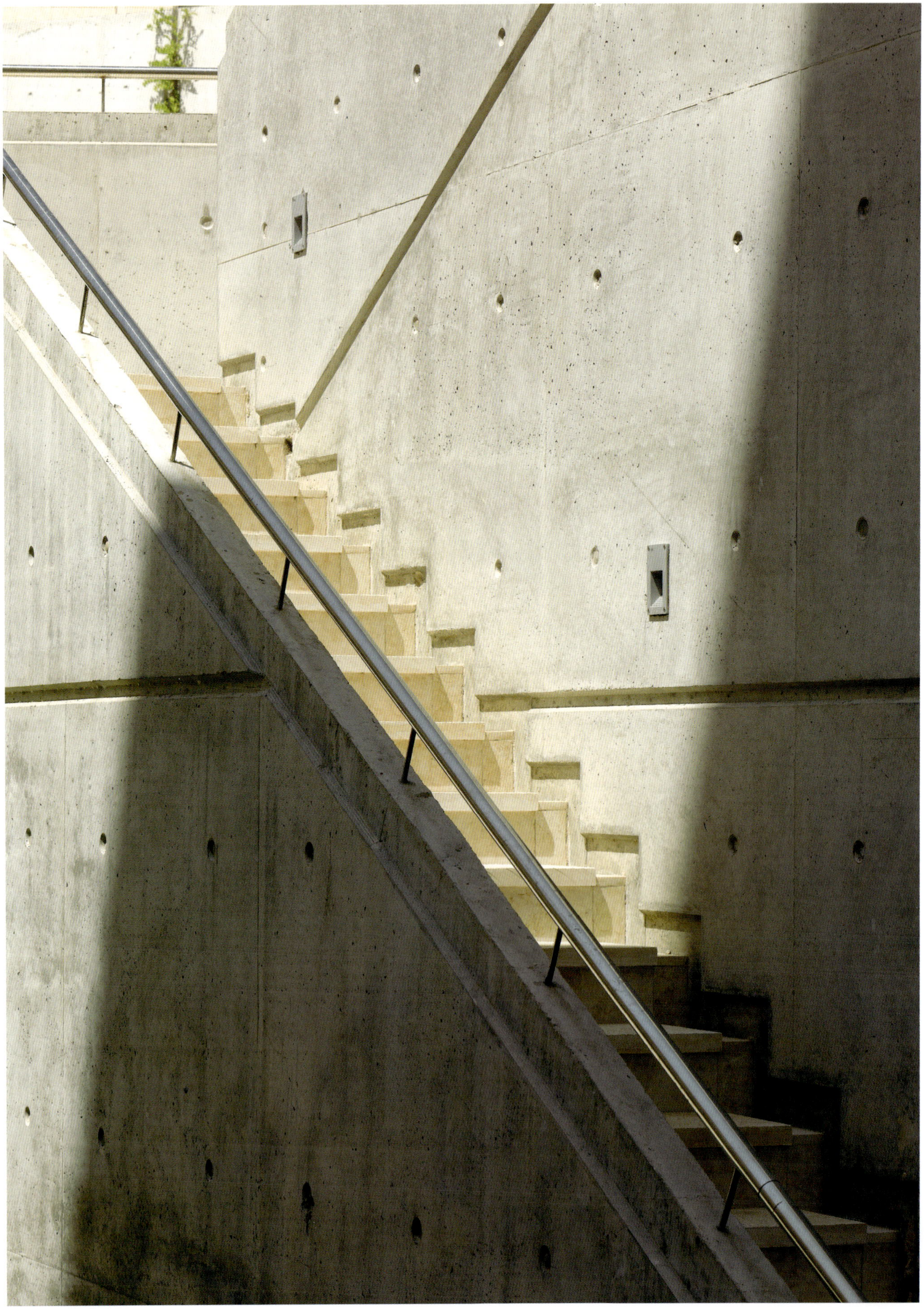

Left:
Stairway leading to the viewing platform above the visitors centre

Right:
Stairway linking faculty offices

Below:
Section through stone stair cantelievered from cast in situ concrete wall

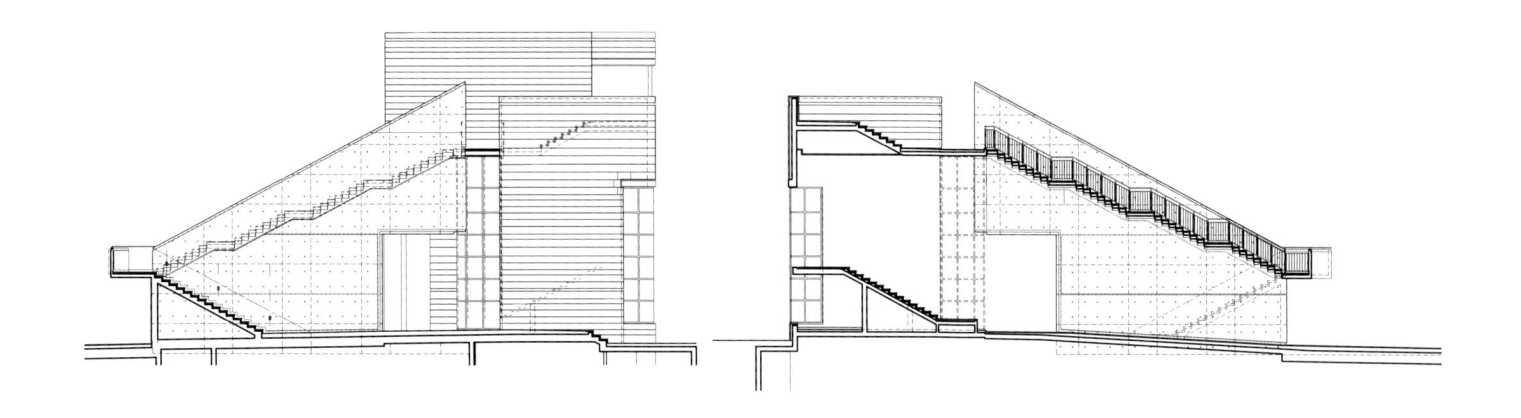

Above:
Stairway leading to the public plaza from the sunken garden

Below:
Decending towards the sunken courtyard of the faculty offices

The approach from the sunken garden towards the public plaza

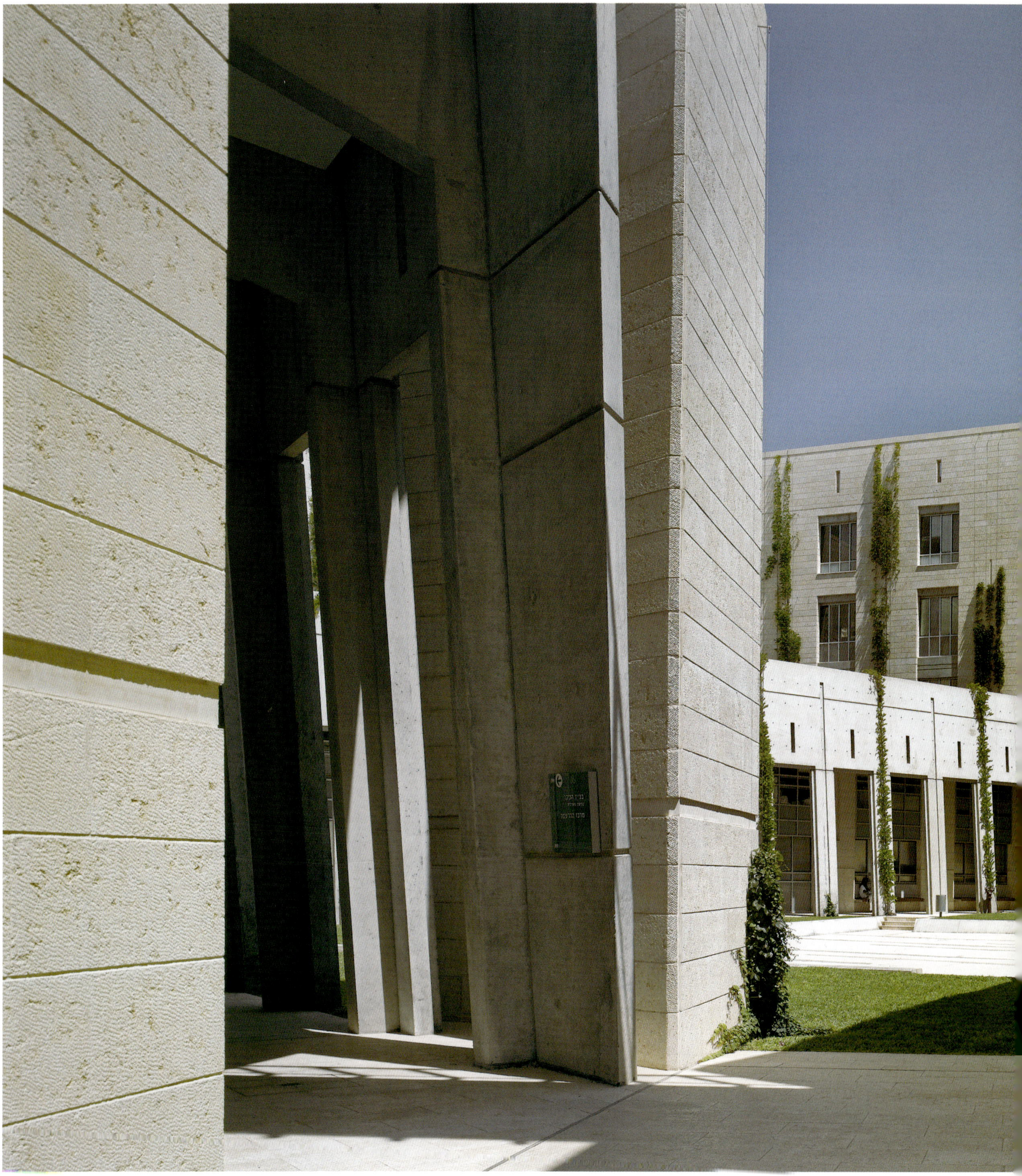

The public plaza surrounded by the arcade and administrative offices

Left:
View of the public plaza from the balcony on the third floor

Right:
View of the cast in situ concrete arcade, surrounding the public plaza

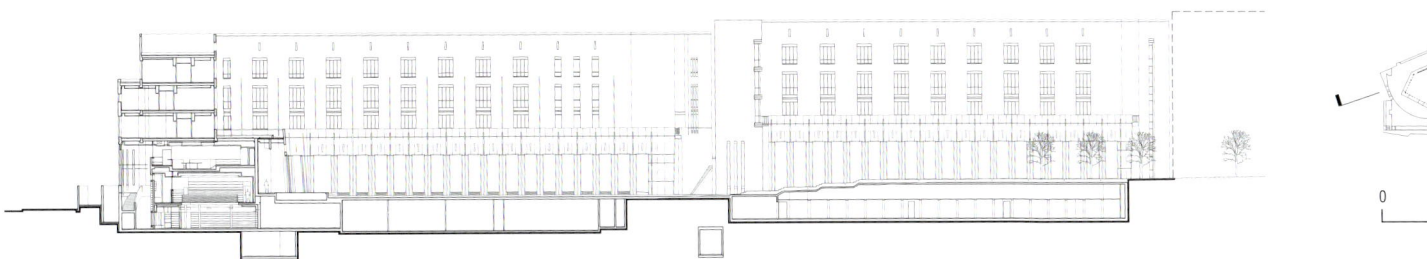

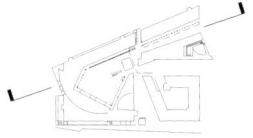

0    25 M

The pedestrain arcade
surrounding the public plaza

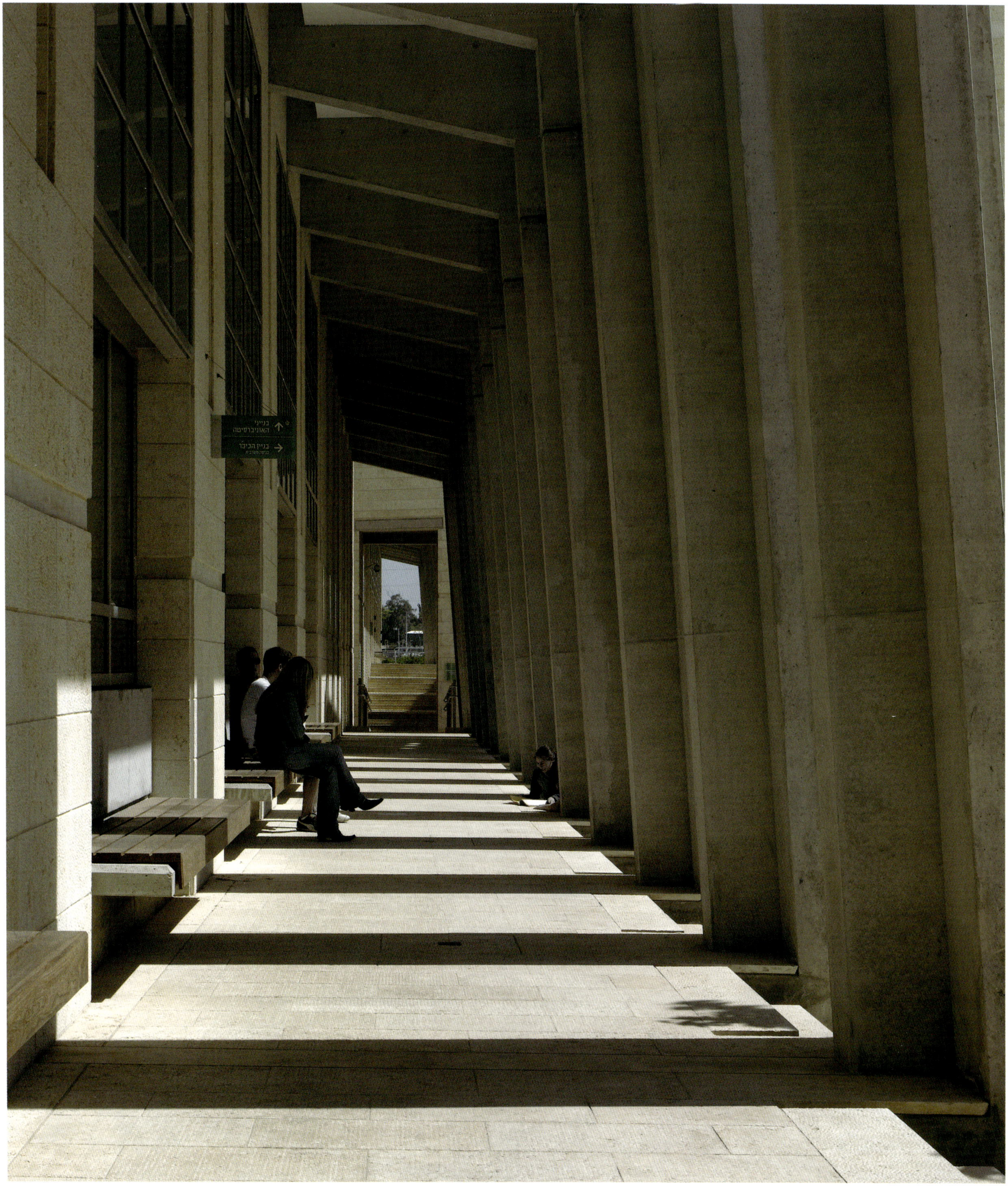
בנייני
האוניברסיטה
בנין הכיכר

58

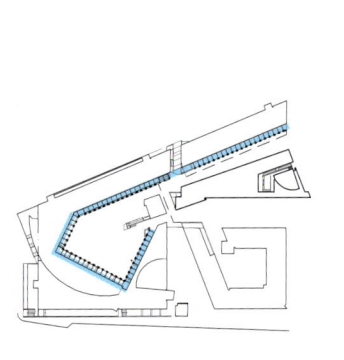

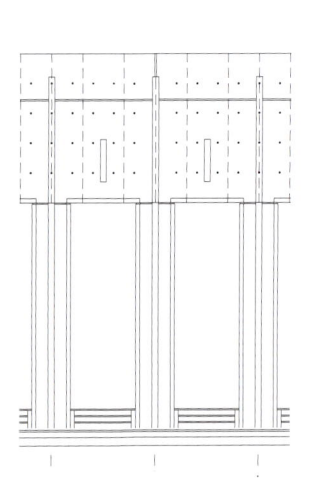

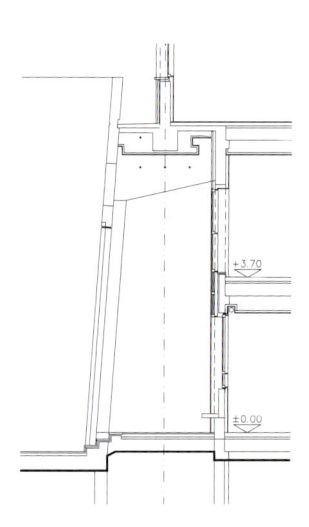

View of the courtyard
and the visitors centre from
the arcade

Above and opposite top:
Detail of the structural cast in situ concrete columns and the stone paving

Stairs leading up to the plaza from the public foyer below

Plan of Public Level
below the Plaza

1. Bookstore
2. Dining hall
3. Large auditorium
4. Small auditorium
5. Public foyer below plaza
6. Library
7. Synagogue
8. Sunken courtyard
9. Faculty offices
10. Stairs up to plaza

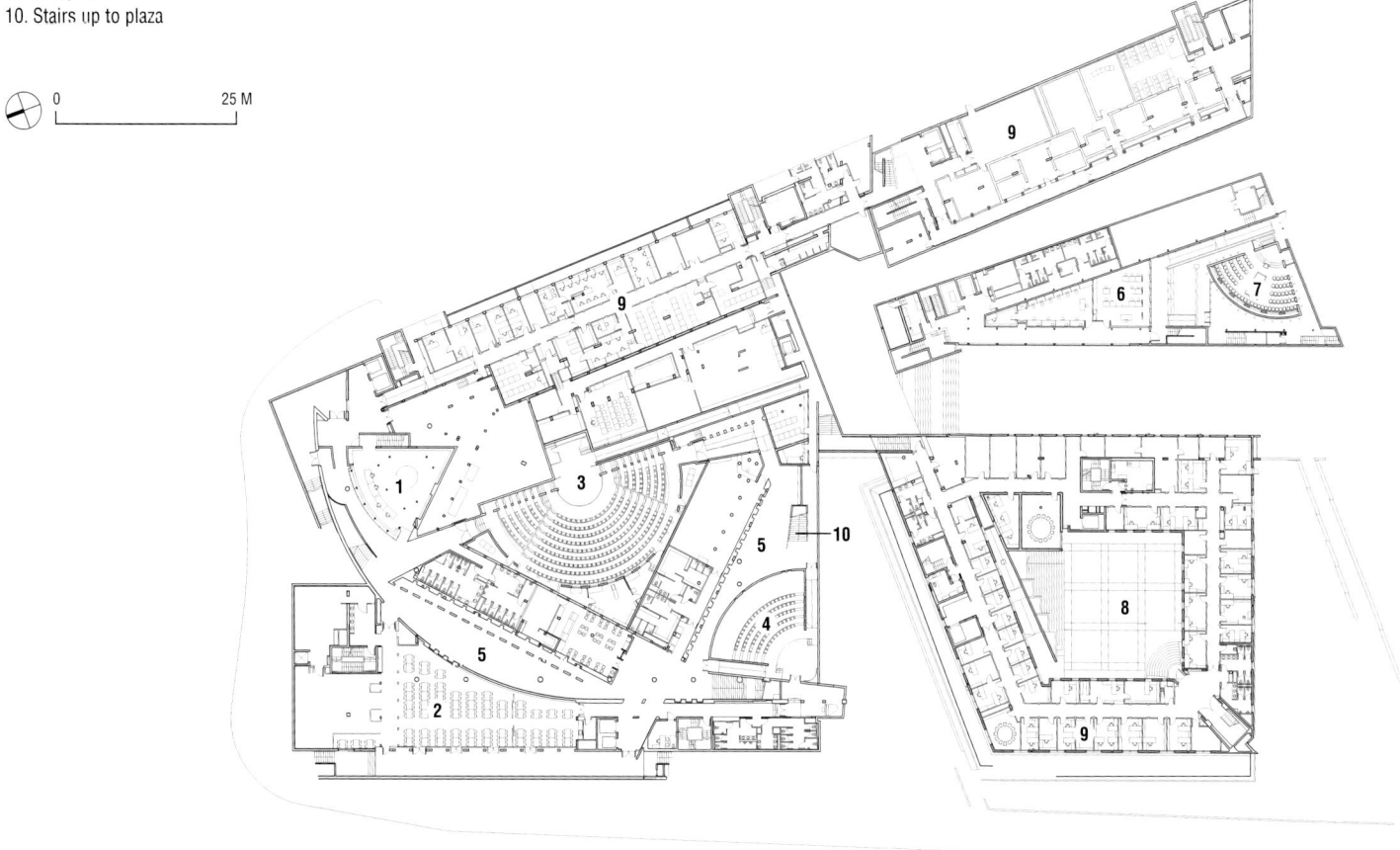

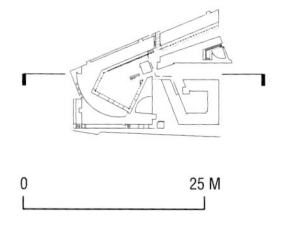

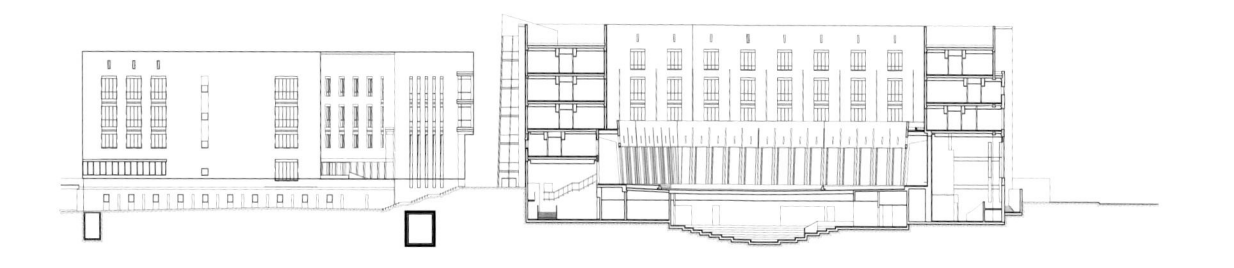

Bookstore

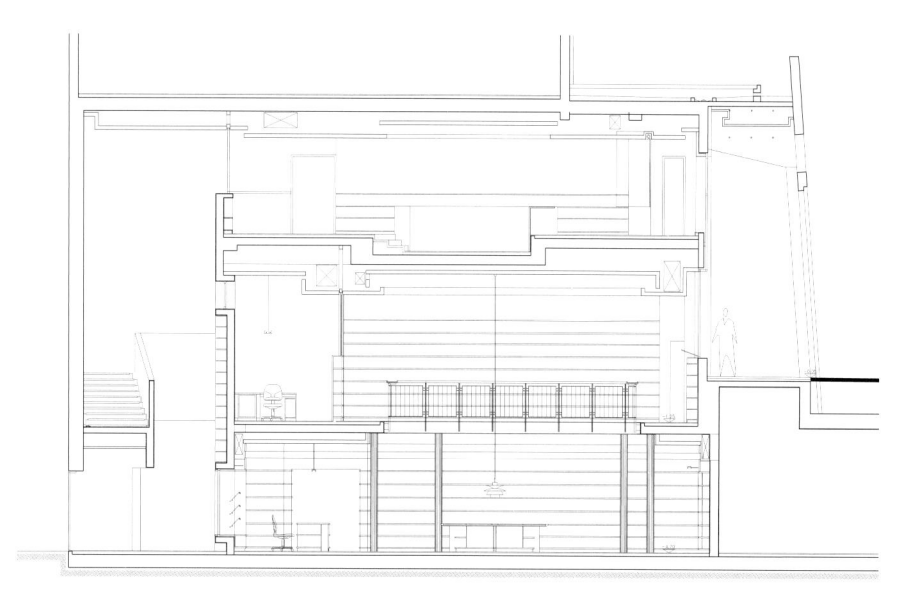

Section through bookstore
and conference room above

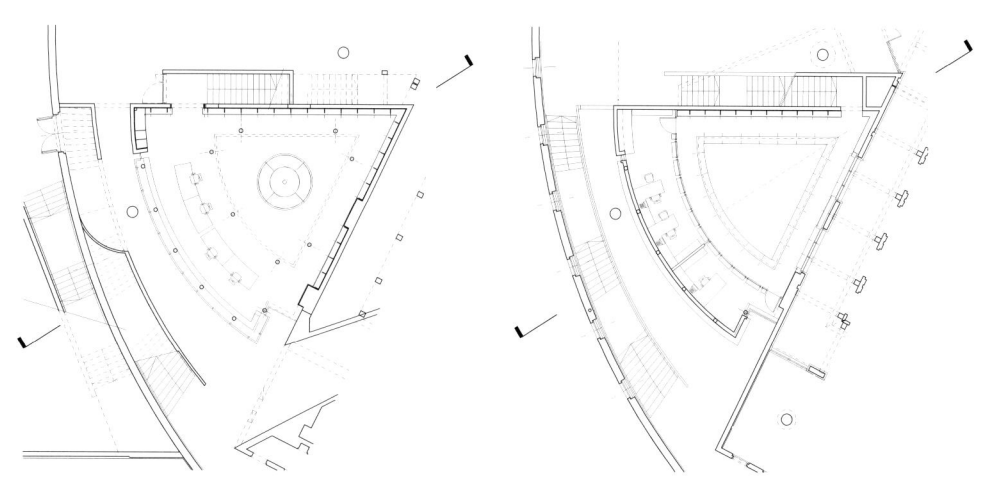

Bookstore: ground floor

Bookstore: gallery

Indirect light decending into
the public foyer

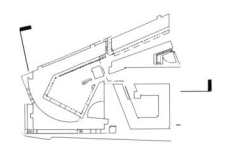

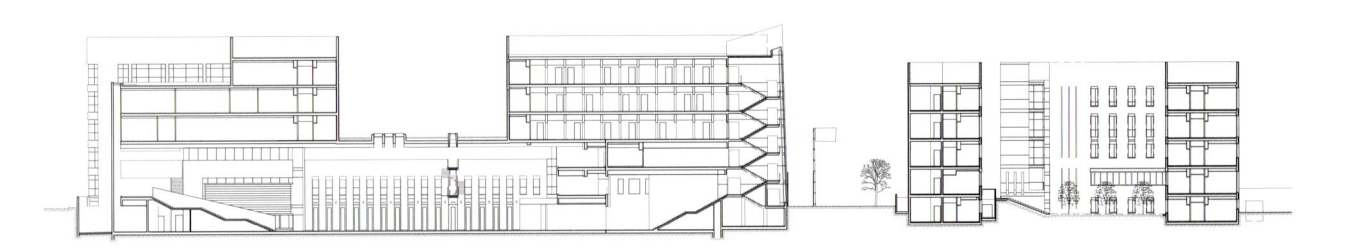

Public foyer below
plaza level

Large auditorium

Small auditorium

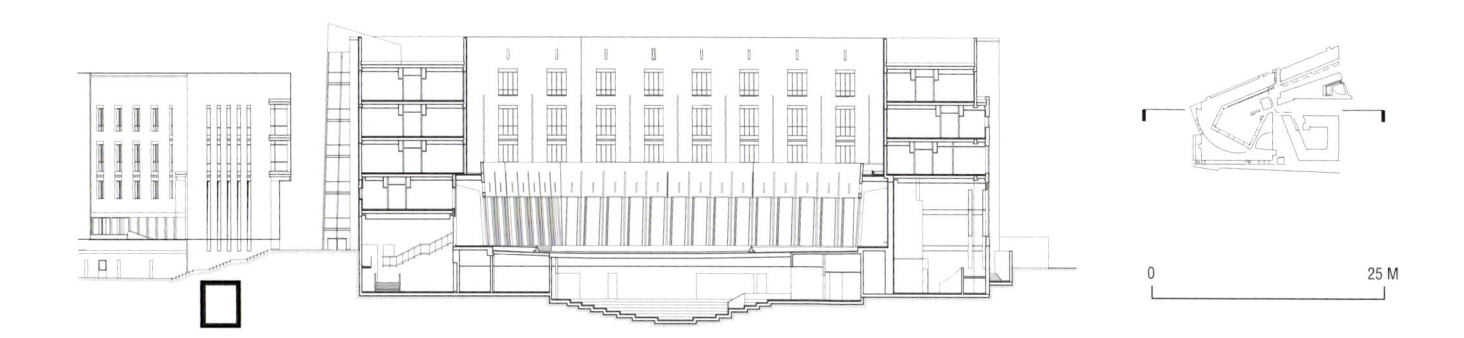

Section through the public plaza
and the auditorium below

0    25 M

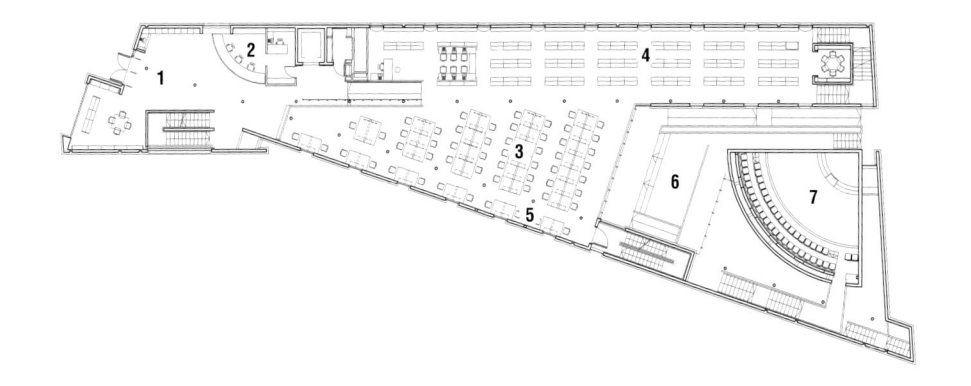

Library Ground Floor Plan

1. Entrance
2. Reception
3. Reading room
4. Stacks
5. Carrels
6. Inner courtyard
7. Synagogue

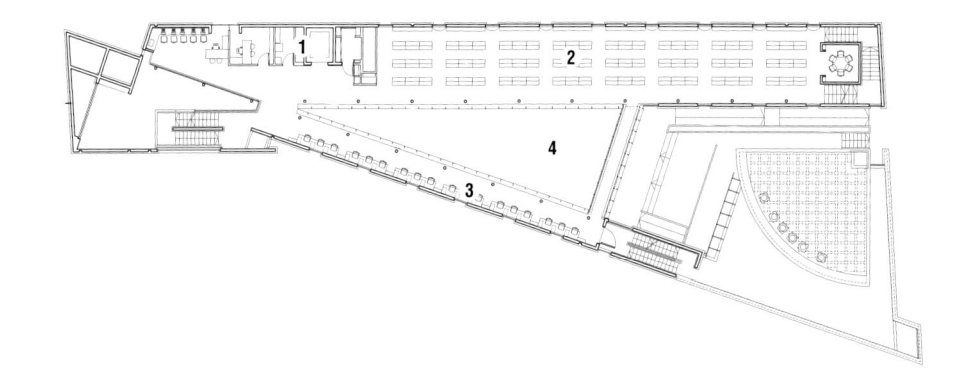

Library First Floor Plan

1. Librarian's office
2. Stacks
3. Carrels
4. Void

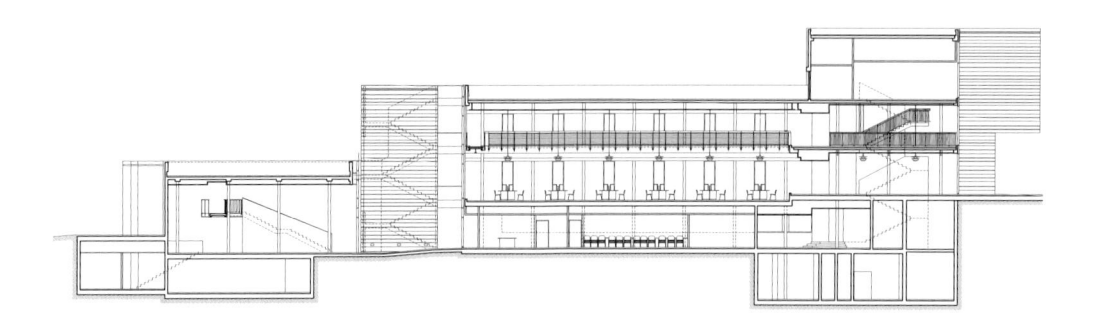

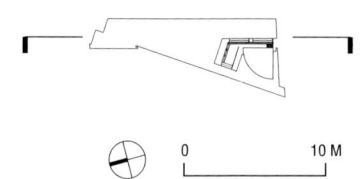

Library

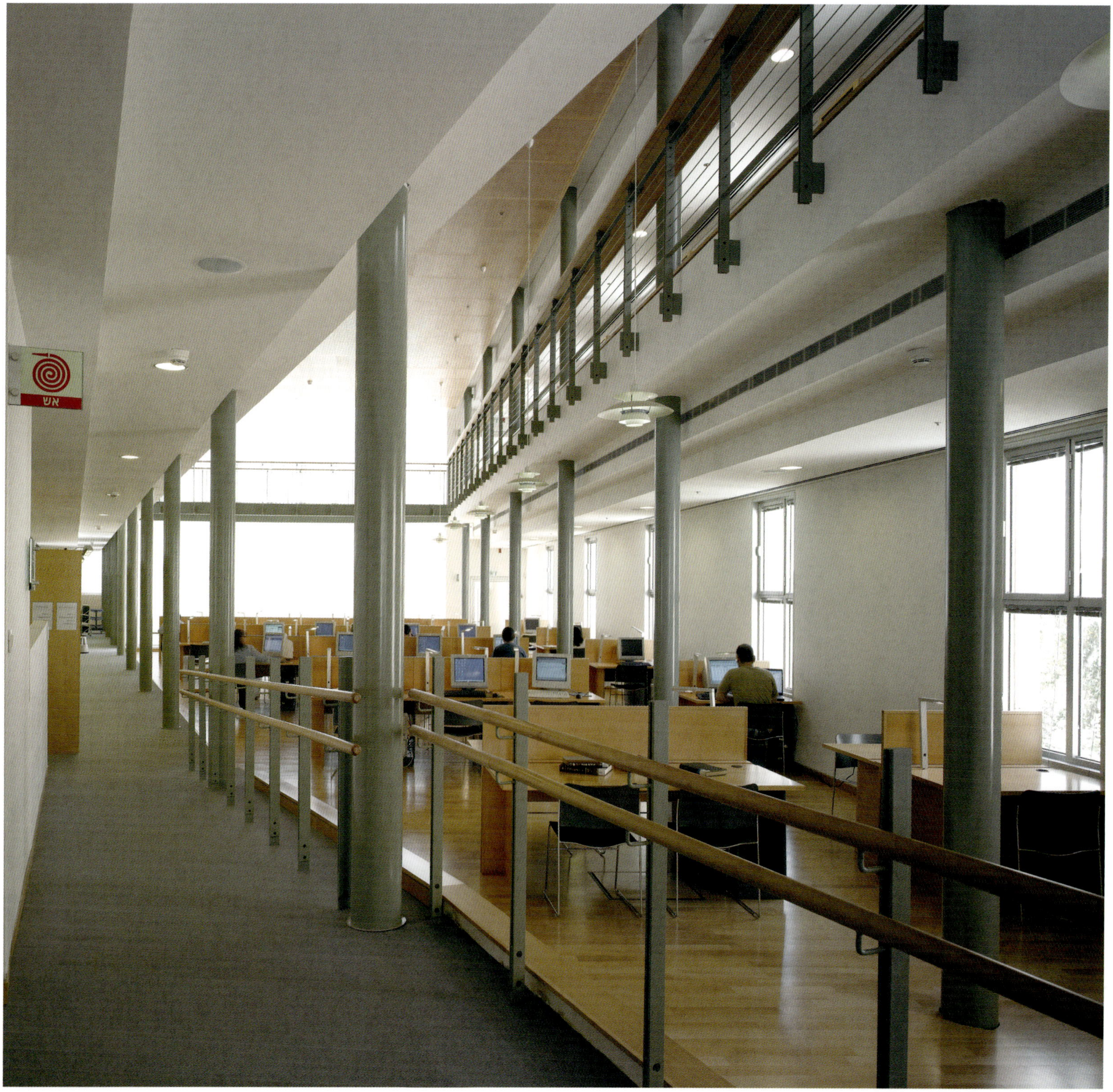
אש

Right:
Detail of railing

Left:
The central reading area

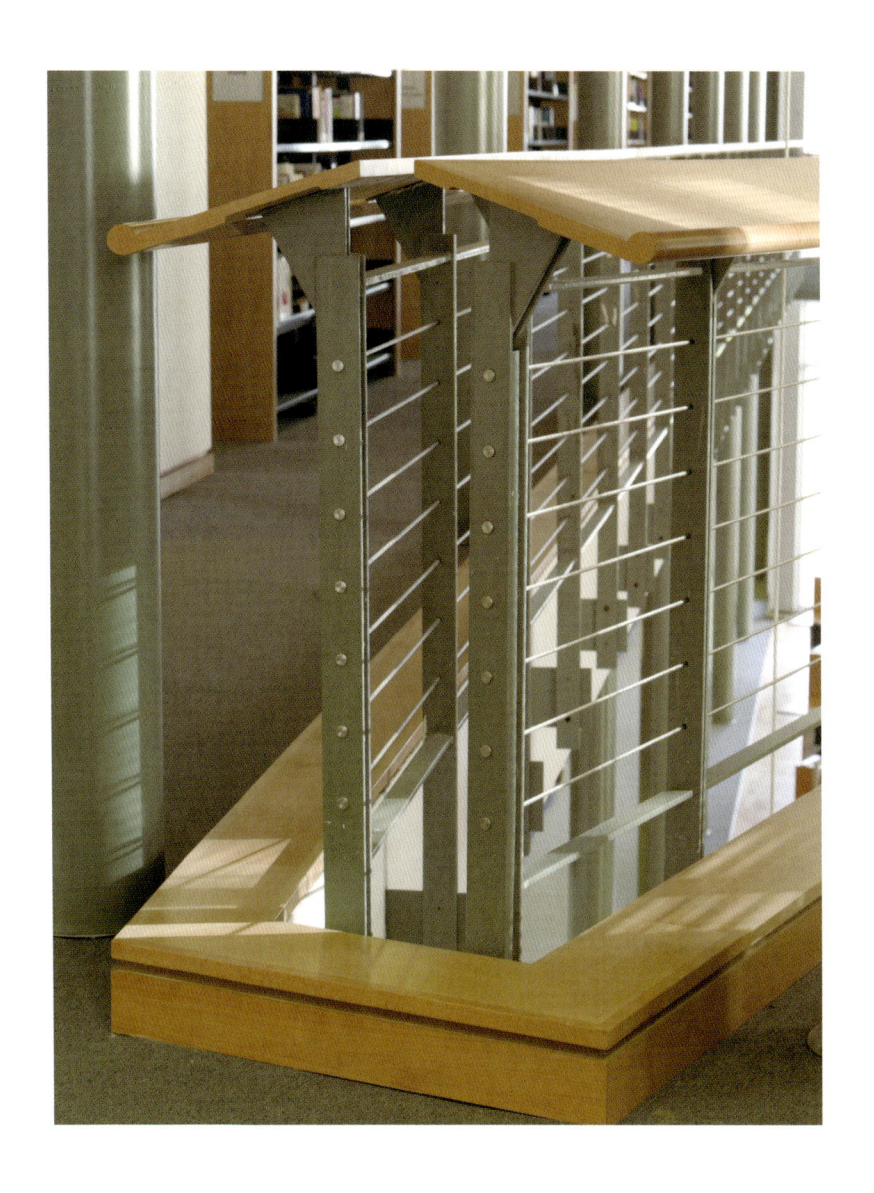

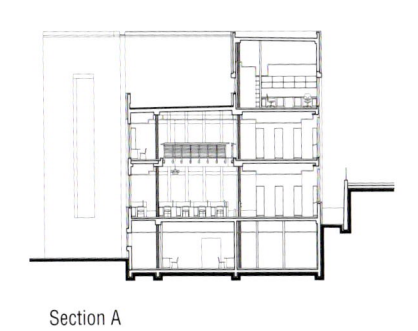

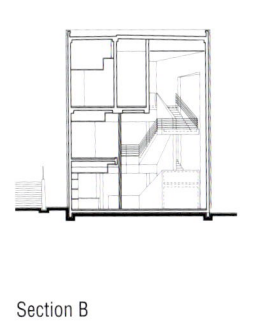

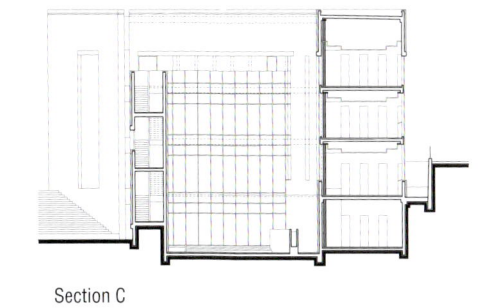

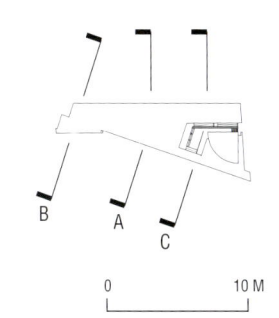

Section A

Section B

Section C

0    10 M

Entrance to the synagogue
and stairs leading to the
women's gallery

View towards the synagogue from the sunken courtyard

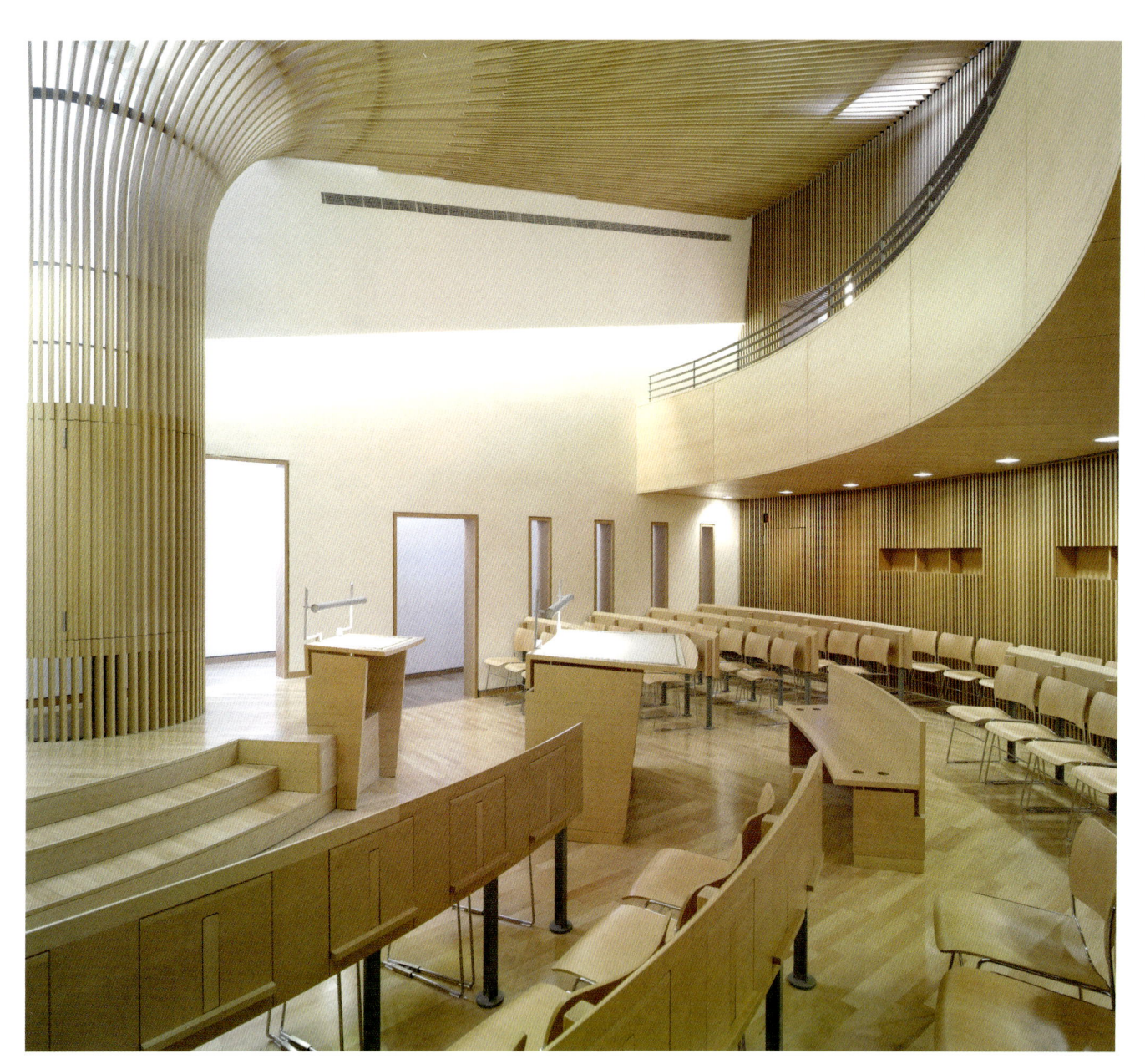

Left:
View of the synagogue interior, the women's gallery and the hung wooden ceiling

Right above:
View from the women's gallery towards the ark

Right below:
View from the ark towards the back wall

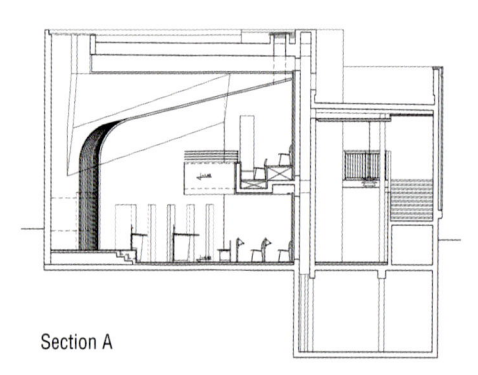

Section A

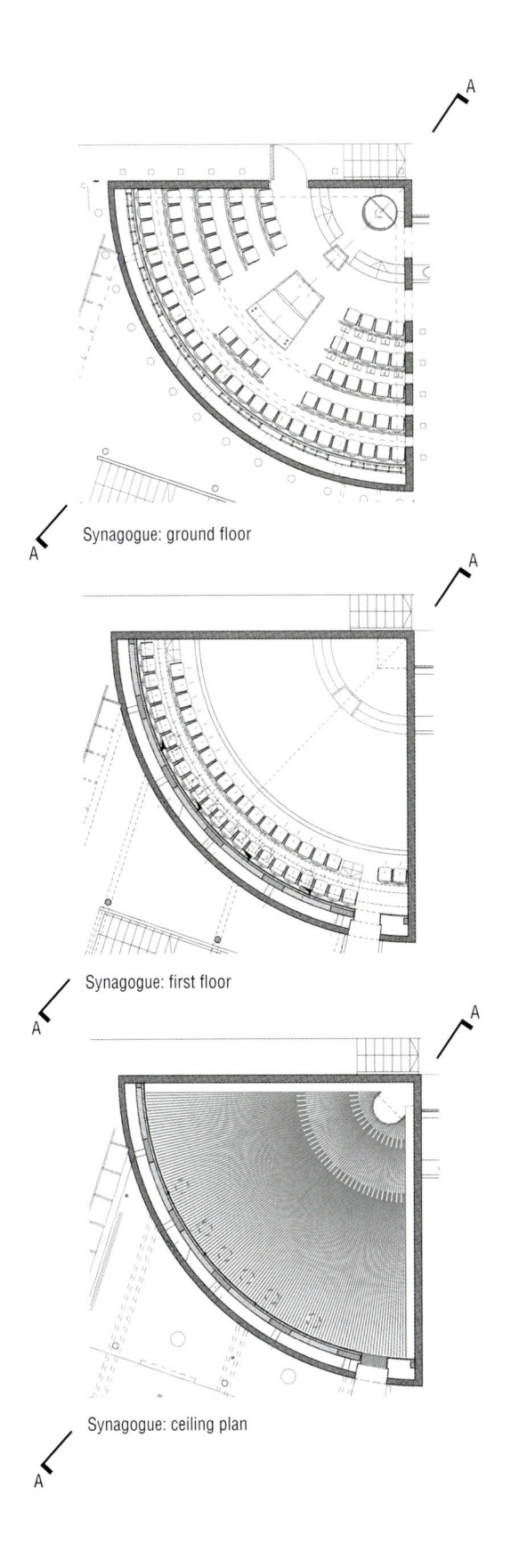

Synagogue: ground floor

Synagogue: first floor

Synagogue: ceiling plan

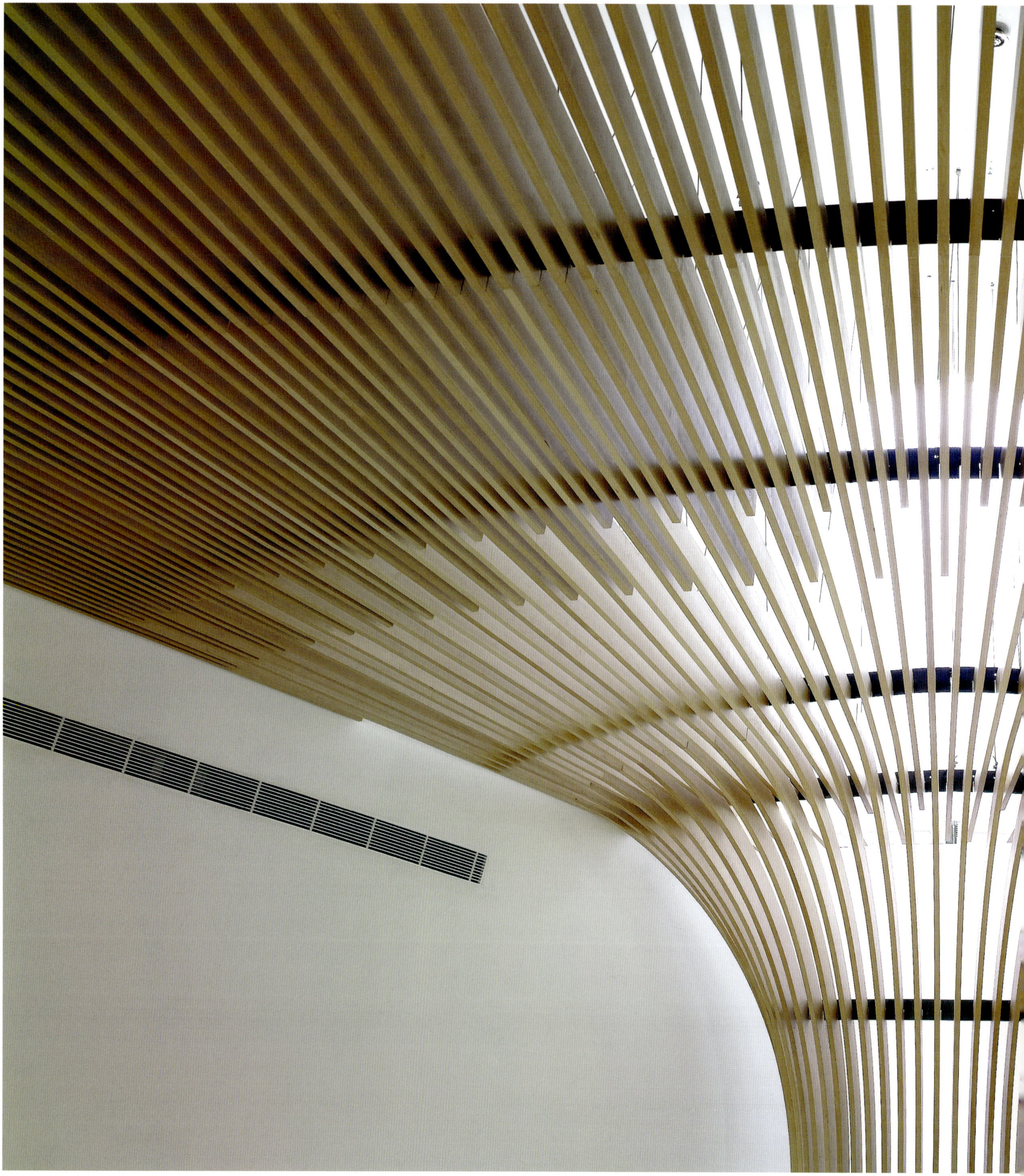

Ceiling detail with light filtering from the top

Second Floor Plan

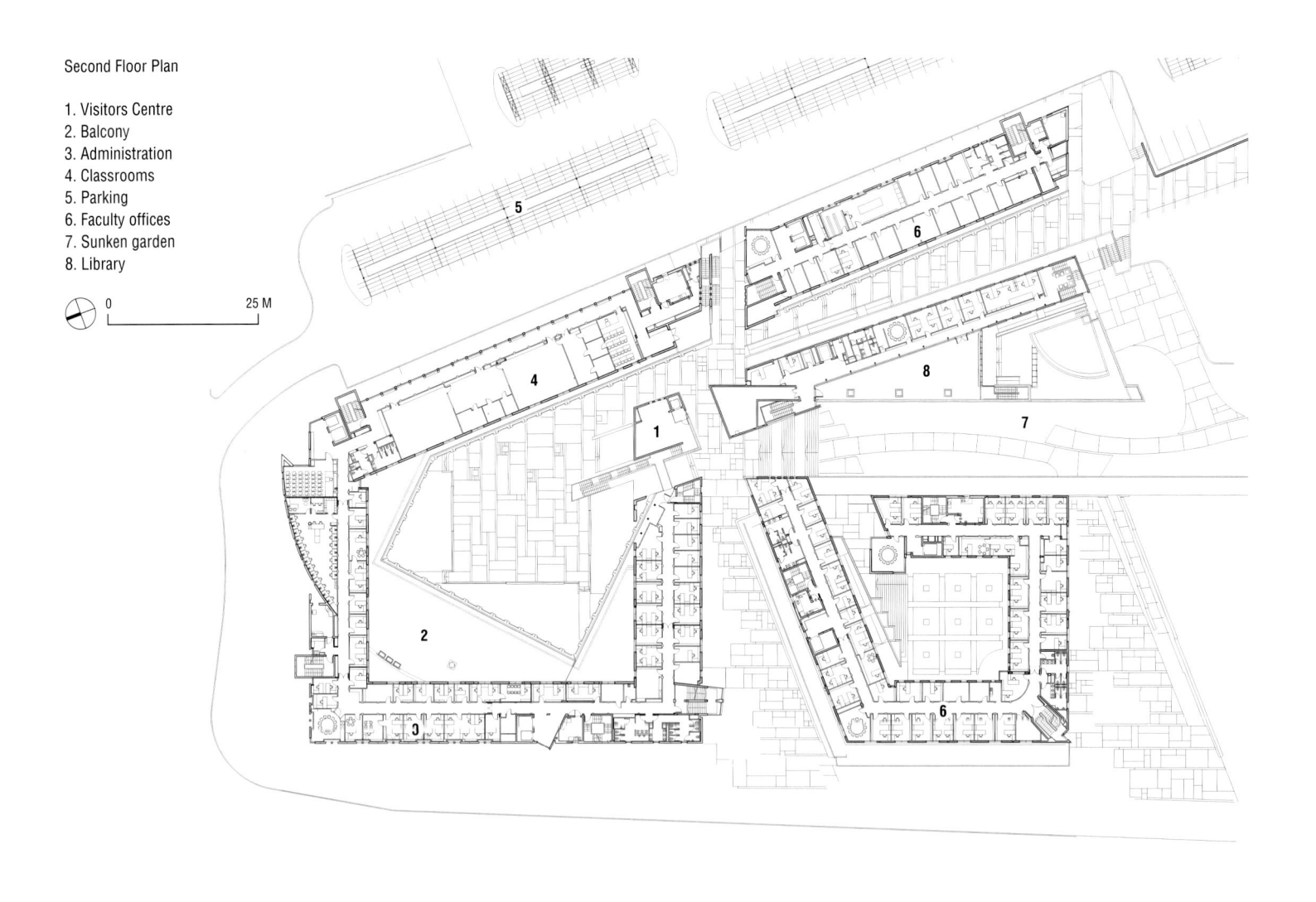

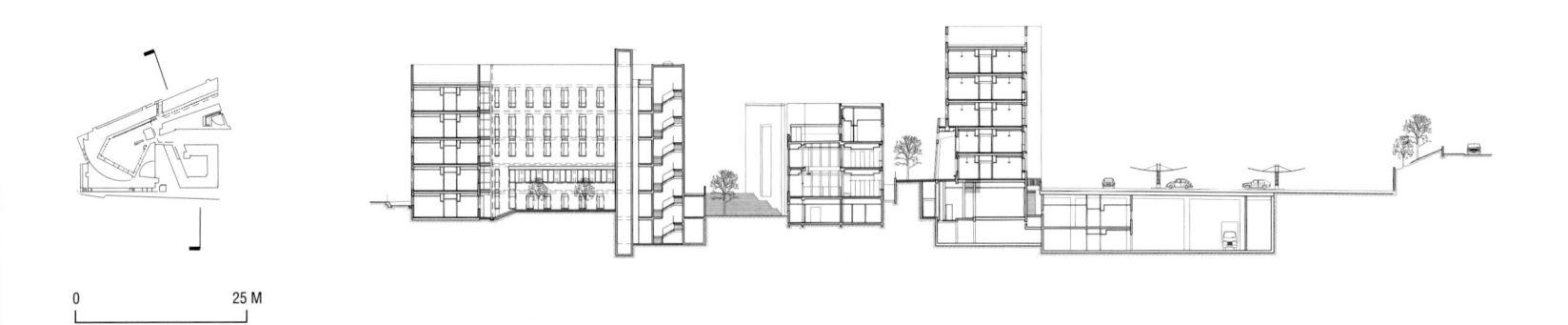

1. Visitors Centre
2. Balcony
3. Administration
4. Classrooms
5. Parking
6. Faculty offices
7. Sunken garden
8. Library

Right:
North elevation

Below left:
Glass Louvers

Below middle:
Internal corridor leading to classrooms

Below right:
East elevation

# The Supreme Court – Jerusalem
Ram Karmi & Ada Karmi-Melamede Architects

North elevation of the Supreme Court, the Knesset and the National Precinct

**The Supreme Court – Jerusalem**
**A Miniature City**

Sketch: public foyer

The first step towards providing a Supreme Court building was taken in the early 1980s, in anticipation of centennial celebrations marking the establishment of the first agricultural colonies in Israel supported by Baron Edmond. Dorothy de Rothschild sought to commemorate this jubilee with a symbolic gesture – the endowment of a building of national significance. Her letters suggest that, prior to his death, her husband had considered providing a building for the Supreme Court or for one of the legislature. His decision, as we know, was to endow the Knesset building. It was Dorothy de Rothschild's belief that a building for the Supreme Court would fully realize her late husband's vision. Her initiative and wisdom turned his vision into a reality.

In 1983, shortly after becoming president of the Supreme Court, Justice Meir Shamgar asked Yad Hanadiv to reconsider its offer. The trustees' preference to locate the court in proximity to the Knesset conformed to Shamgar's own conception that Kiryat Ben-Gurion, the Government, or National Precinct of Jerusalem, should house all three branches of government: judicial, executive and legislative.

In response, on 19 December 1984 Dorothy de Rothschild sent a letter to Prime Minister Shimon Peres (who had succeeded Yitzhak Shamir), formally renewing the offer of a new Supreme Court building. With her usual modesty, she defined her role as a merely ensuring that the building be completed in accordance with her husband's wishes and in the spirit of his earlier bequest. 'We see our response to the need for a new Supreme Court building as a development of the work of both my husband and of his father before him.'

She wrote: 'The aim of both was to provide some of the essentials needed by the people of Israel since the days of the first Aliyah. These ideals still animate our Foundation and will I trust continue to inspire future generations to come.'

Arthur Fried, Yad Hanadiv's Israel-based trustee, in close consultation with Lord Rothschild, was responsible for the project. He carefully followed the design and construction process and was involved in selecting a professional team to supervise the project: engineers Dan Wind and Eliezer Rahat, general contractor Gabriel Peretz and many technical consultants. Two of his decisions were particularly crucial. The first was to select a site on the ridge of Givat Ram, and not on its eastern slope as originally proposed by the government. The second was to invite architects Ada Karmi-Melamede and Ram Karmi to participate as a team in the 1986 architectural competition. Arthur Fried turned to the two, even though the brother-and-sister architects had never submitted a joint proposal to an architectural competition.

Their winning entry is a unique and singular story. They developed their concept in the broadest scope, including interior design, furnishing details and landscaping.

The building's exterior combines features of traditional local architecture with contemporary concepts. The massive stone walls and detailed work relieve the observer, at least momentarily, of the vagueness of the Israeli identity, as reflected in the country's modern architecture. The building is firmly rooted, both historically and stylistically, in Jerusalem, and not merely in the Government Precinct.

Every leading architect who has built in Jerusalem (Mendelsohn, Harrison, Holiday) has fallen under the city spell. In their statement of intent, Karmi-Melamede and Karmi cited the need to make the building a part of the city's cultural and historical context. Their intention was that design transcend vagaries of style and history.

Karmi-Melamede and Karmi's plan, based on a horizontal massing, best adapted itself

**South elevation and axis to the Knesset**

to the ridge. It also fulfilled the important stipulation in the competition brief that equal weight be accorded to the Knesset building, situated to the south of the Supreme Court.

The building's elevations are stark and simple. The north façade is perceived as a city wall and yet the formal expression of the building does not lend itself to unequivocal classification. The structure consists of four distinct parts (library, courtrooms, judges' chambers and parking area), each symmetrical in itself and linked by a major flowing space. The building evokes ancient structures like Absalom's Tomb in the Kidron Valley, synagogues and Byzantine churches, while paying homage to the Rockefeller Museum and the arched vaults of Government House (the seat of the high commissioner of Palestine during the British Mandate).

For appellants and petitioners, the new building, like its predecessor in the Russian Compound, is a place entered by necessity, although it merits a visit solely for the architectural experience. The architect's original plan for a building divided into four parts and including a spacious public level pre-empted a palatial structure. The law as a normative principle in both individual and public life was the architects' main consideration, the building accords it great respect.

The long entrance leading to the courtrooms, and the stepped transition from the Jerusalem exterior to the building's interior, start as an alley and develop into a large public domain. This sequence suggests the complex affiliations to archaic motifs, to Jerusalem elements and to the Israeli landscape. The architects sought to internalize and express the needs of the building's permanent resident, the Supreme Court, and perhaps even more, the expectations of the Israeli public.

The schematic design stage for the Supreme Court building explored many alternatives before a concept was selected for development. The initial approach was largely determined by the existence of three axis which intersect the site. The first, is the north–south axis running along the ridge of the hill which connects the Central Bus Station, the Convention Center, the Hilton Hotel, the Parliament and The Israel Museum. This axis, the most formal of the three, serves as the major public approach to the government complex. The second is a green east–west axis that connects Sacher Park, Wohl Rose Park and the Hebrew University's Givat Ram Campus. The third is an emerging axis, already evident in the urban fabric, which extends between the old city and the National Precinct. It will eventually connect The Rockefeller Museum to the Wohl Park, stringing together many important public spaces. Once this axis is formally articulated, it will strengthen not only the ties between the old and new parts of the city, but also those between its spiritual and secular institutions. By incorporating these axes into the scheme, the building acts as a single, freestanding object in the landscape, which relates both to its immediate environment and to the larger urban context. The building was intentionally positioned at their intersection in order to reinforce the relationship between the executive, legislative, and judicial branches of the government and to create a public space common to all three.

West elevation and view of the Wohl Rose Park

The Supreme Court building is composed of four seemingly autonomous parts: the library, the courtrooms, the judges' chambers and the parking structure. They are separated by the north–south and east–west axes of superimposed and intersecting movement that extend throughout the building. Although the building does not have an imposing entrance, it is designed to receive throngs of visitors. Neither the location of the entrance nor the approach to it is obtrusive. From afar, the portal projects moderate strength and authority – owning partly to the fact that it is not centred on a symmetrical front. Conspicuously absent are steep steps leading to the entrance – a conventional symbol of authority.

From the entrance, one ascends a grand stairway similar to a Jerusalem stone alley towards a curved glass curtain wall at the 'public level' (on which all administrative services are located) where a panoramic view of the city is revealed. The space beneath the pyramid beyond acts as the inner 'gatehouse' to the Supreme Court and serves as a turning point after which one encounters the actual entrance hall. The pure pyramid form tapers toward the apex allowing a column of light to penetrate. The library, because of its important function housing the collective memory of the law, which was historically located at the 'gatehouse', is tiered about this space and is defined by a curved façade, a continuation of the large curved window.

The wing comprising the courtrooms is separated from that of the judges' chambers and administrative offices, so as to differentiate between the place of public hearings and the place of contemplation and deliberation. The judges' chambers, each opening to a private patio overlooking the city to the east or to the Knesset axis to the west, envelope an internal arcaded courtyard, which forms a quiet place that allows for seclusion and introspection.

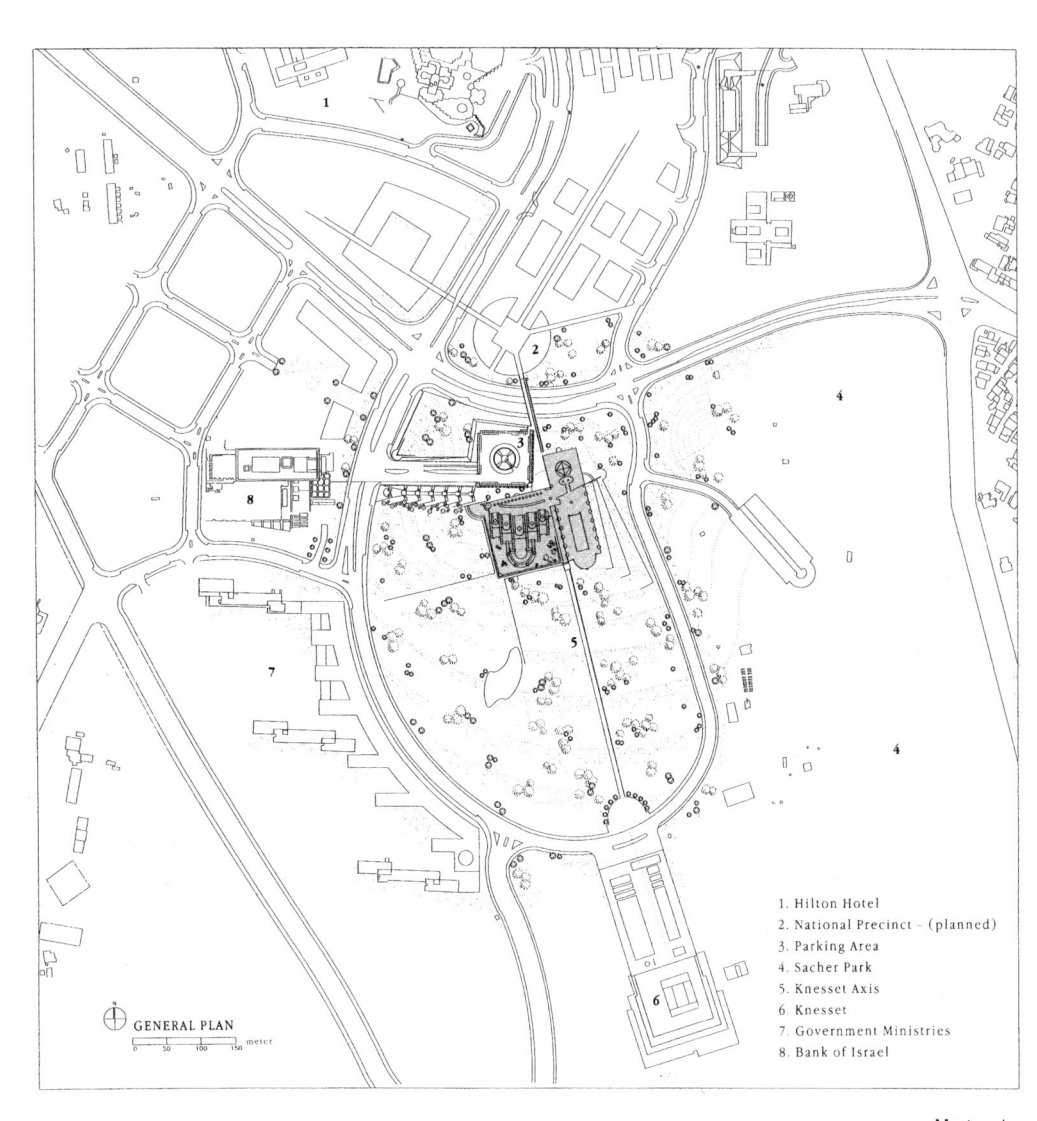

1. Hilton Hotel
2. National Precinct – (planned)
3. Parking Area
4. Sacher Park
5. Knesset Axis
6. Knesset
7. Government Ministries
8. Bank of Israel

Master plan

The judges descend to the courtrooms, the public enters at the courtroom level while the accused, if any, ascend from below. The courtrooms appear to be set in niches formed by the natural terrain. They are faced inside with smooth stone in contrast to the roughness of the outside retaining walls. The courtrooms are designed to separate the outer shell from the inner room. Natural light of varying intensity filters down between these two layers. In contrast to the brilliant light of the courtyard, the reflected light within the courtrooms is soft and tranquil.

The transition from one section of the building to the next takes place through a grand and dynamic circulation pattern, starting at the entrance level and proceeding to the courtrooms above. This movement is perceived to be a fragment of a longer

Sketch: entrance sequence

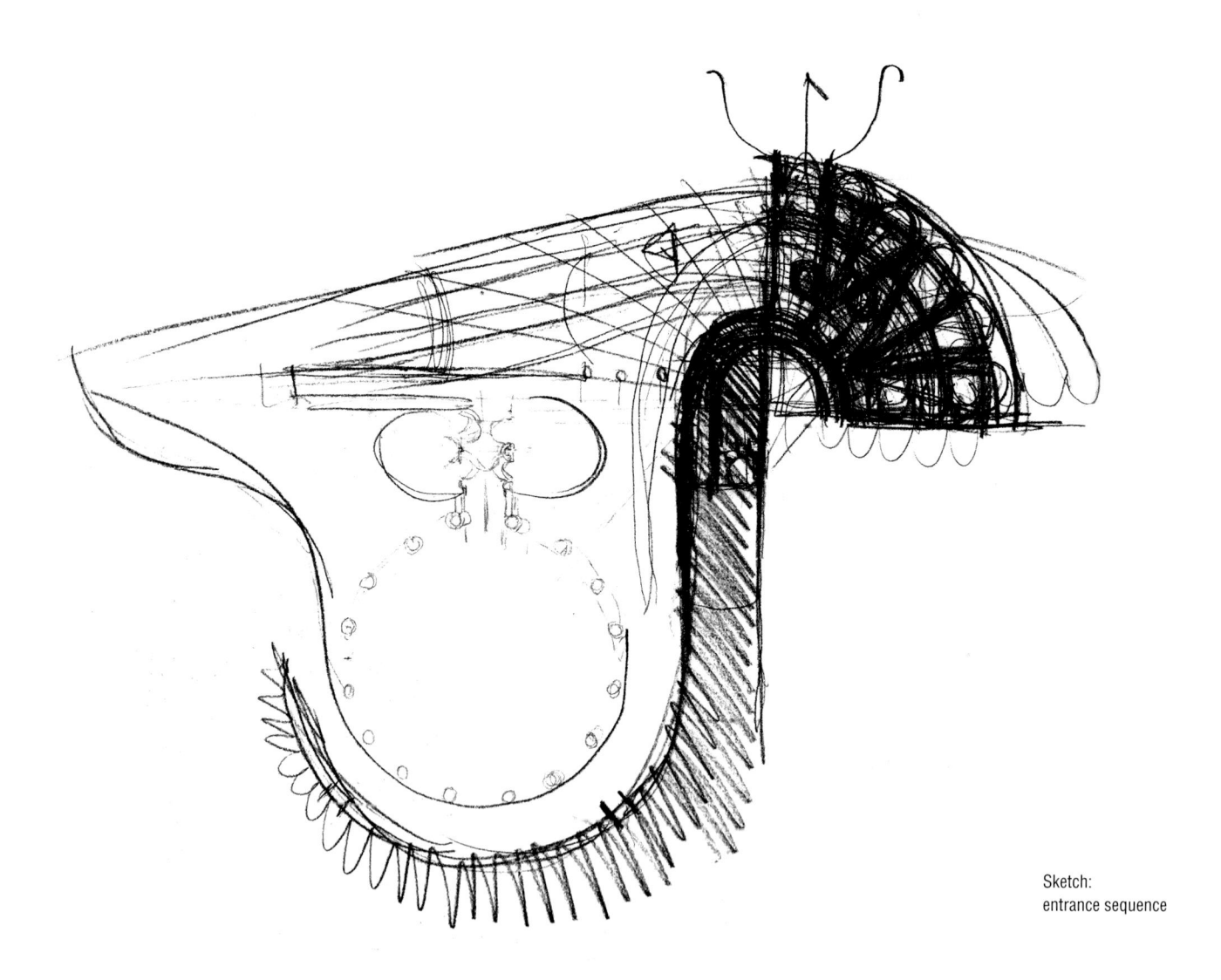

route in which architectural space mediates between the time and language of today and that of the past. Thus, the procession within the building becomes part of a greater process, whereby the simple order of the structure is experienced as intricate and complex.

The stone façades are not uniform. They carefully preserve memories of historic Jerusalem, a miniature city enclosed by a wall. And yet, they uncover a new and different reality of a more liberated geometry articulated in white plaster planes.

In distancing itself from the stone face of the external wall, light wells of different shapes and sizes are dispersed throughout the building. These voids transform raw light into human light, allowing it to be reflected in a palate of shades. The sequence of movement is followed and enhanced by a sequence of light patterns.

*Yossi Sharon*

Entrance Level
Ground Floor

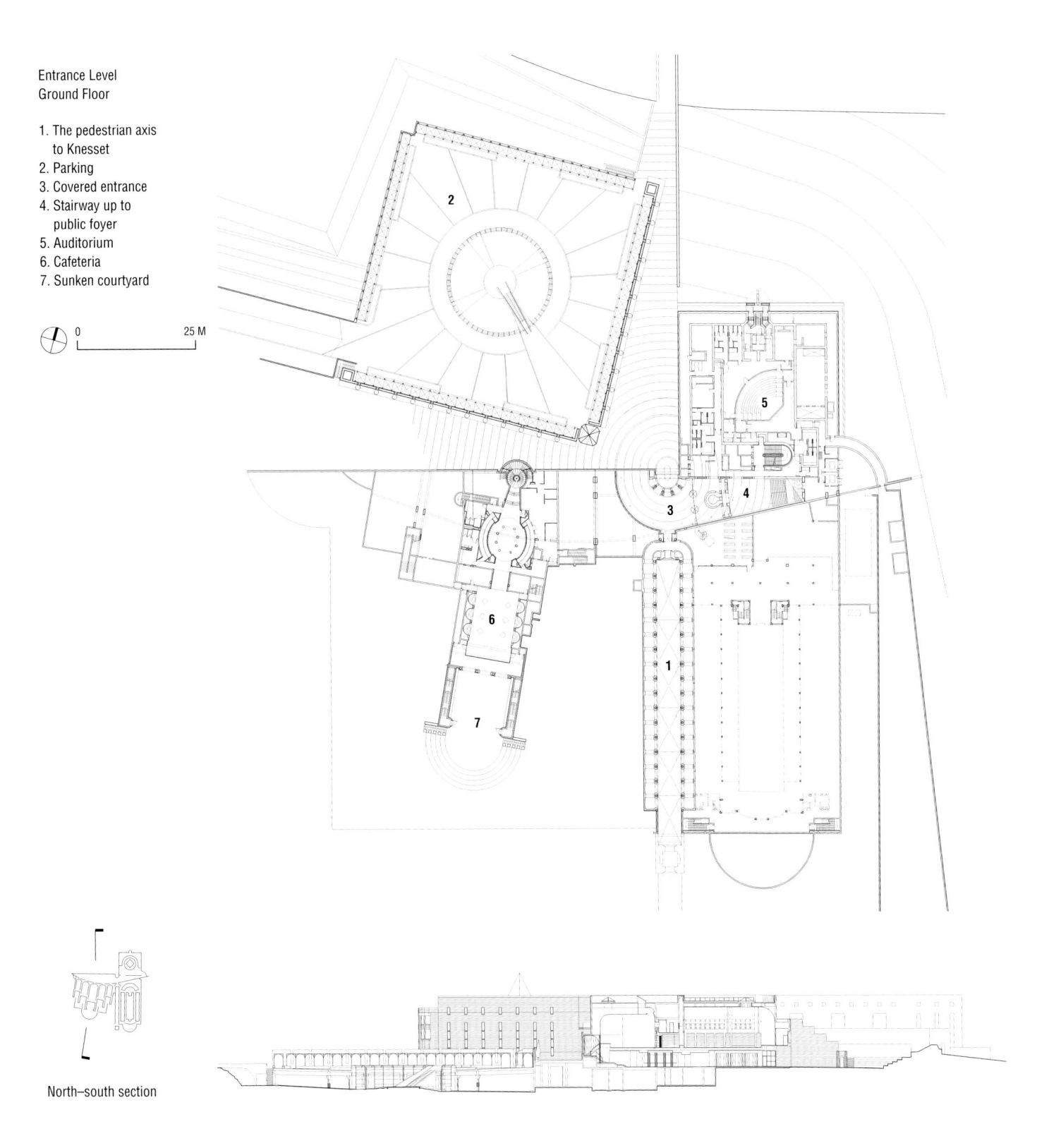

1. The pedestrian axis to Knesset
2. Parking
3. Covered entrance
4. Stairway up to public foyer
5. Auditorium
6. Cafeteria
7. Sunken courtyard

North–south section

The Public Foyer:
First Floor

1. Window facing Jerusalem
2. The 'Tent': the elevated 'gatehouse'
3. Library
4. Administration
5. Public foyer
6. Courtrooms
7. Stairway to the cafeteria below

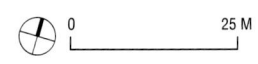

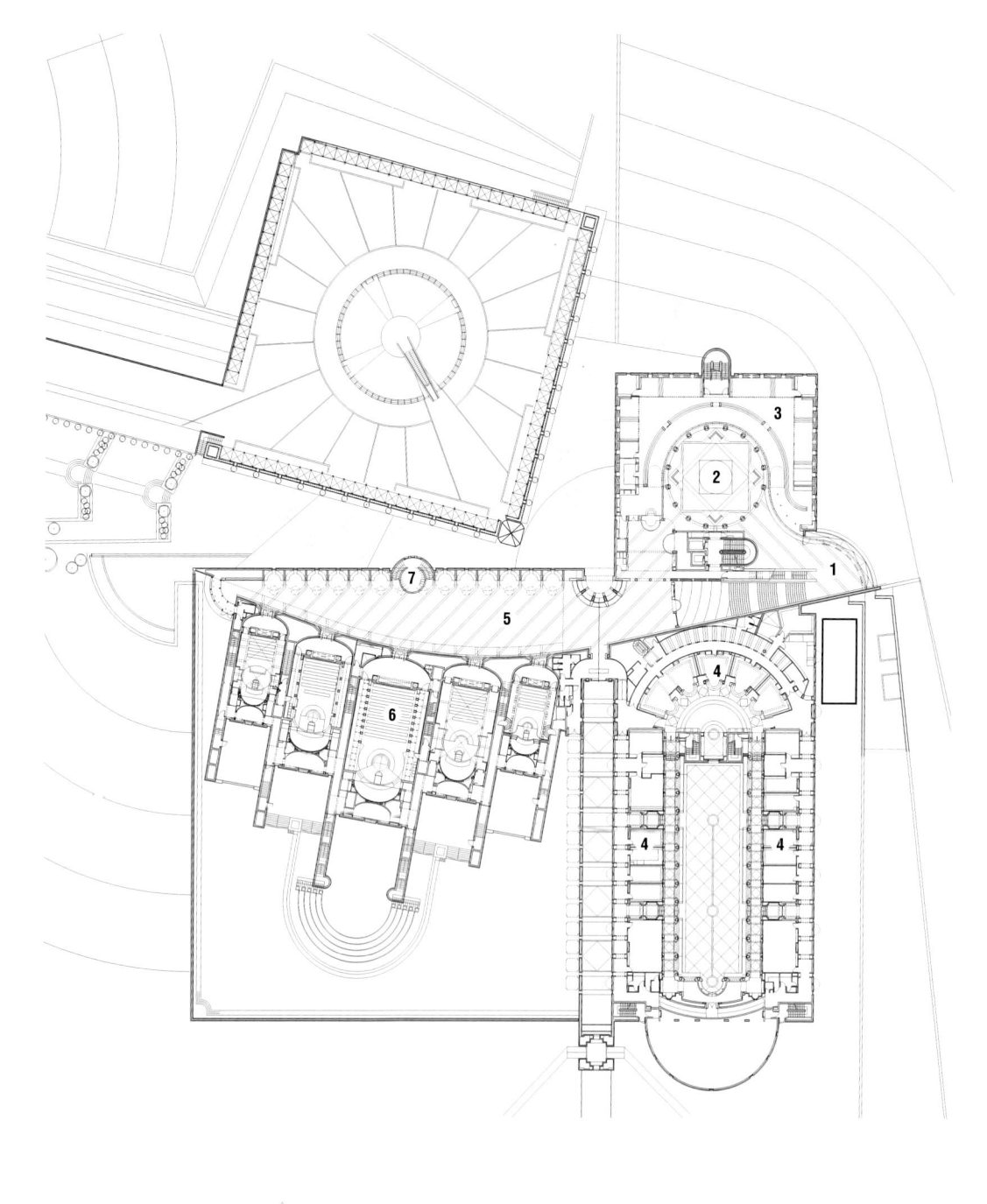

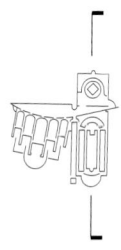

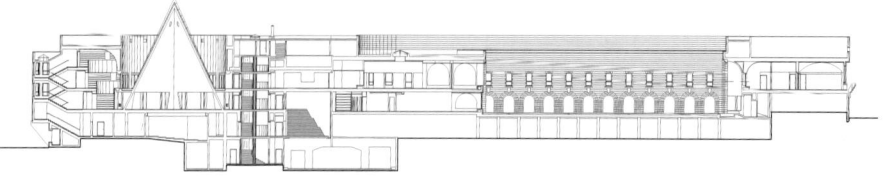

North–south section

The Judges' Level:
Second Floor

1. Judges' chambers
2. Chief Justice's chamber
3. Judges' corridor and stairs leading to courtrooms
4. Library

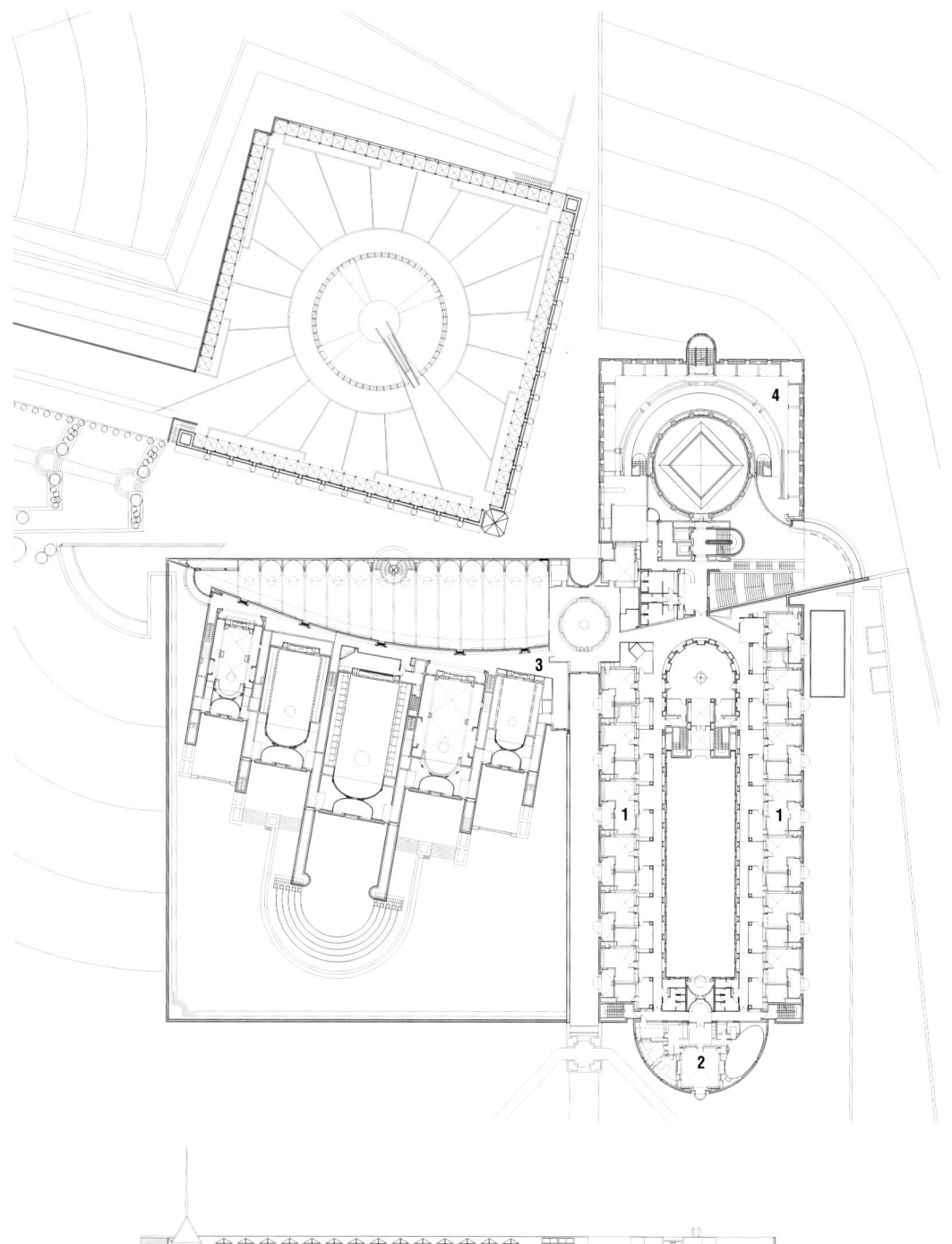

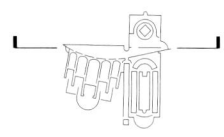

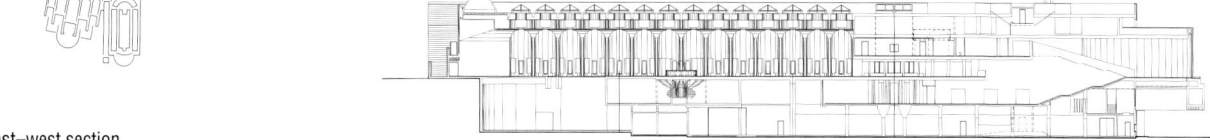

0    25 M

East–west section

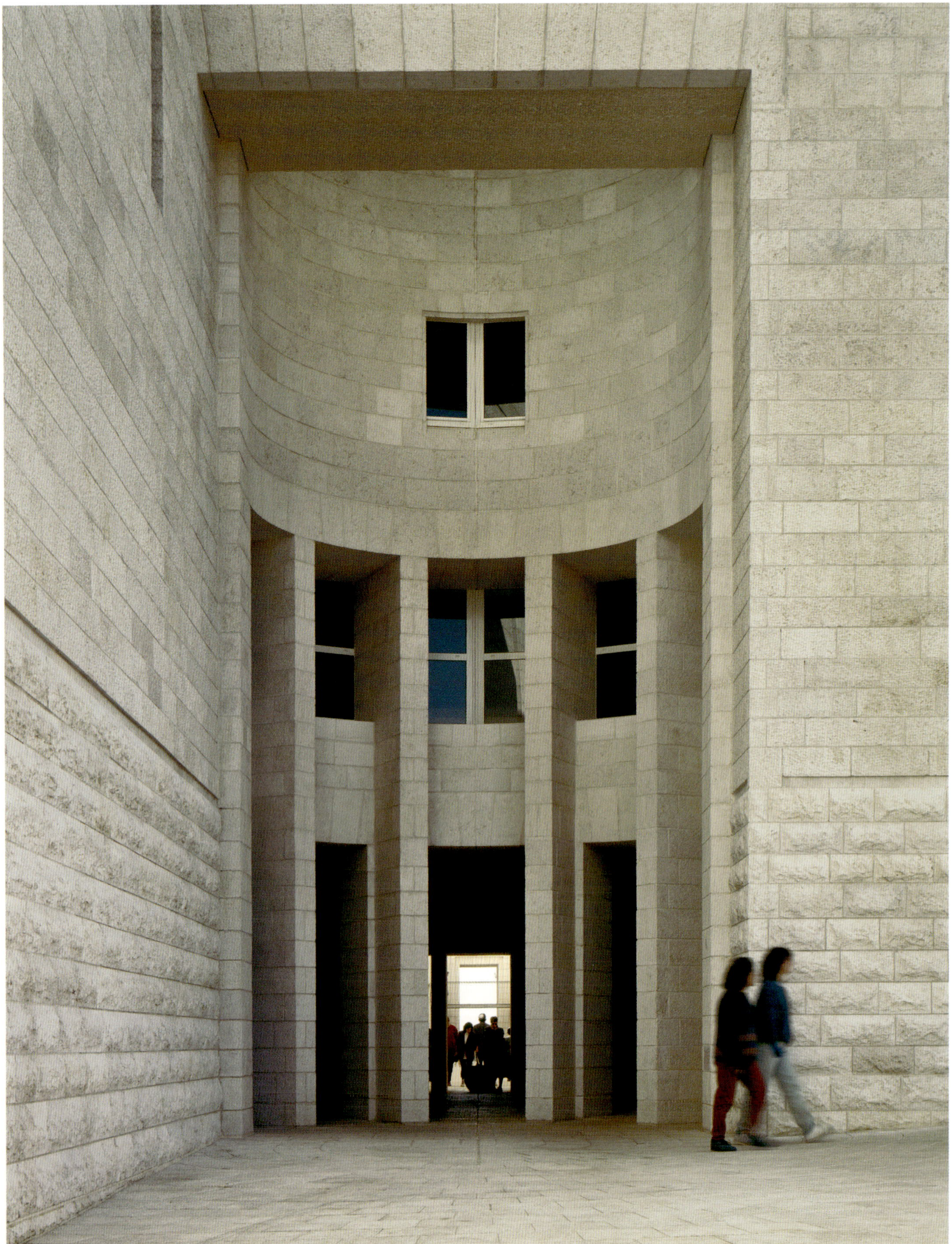

Right:
Sketch: entrance 'gate'

Left & below right:
Main entrance to the Supreme Court

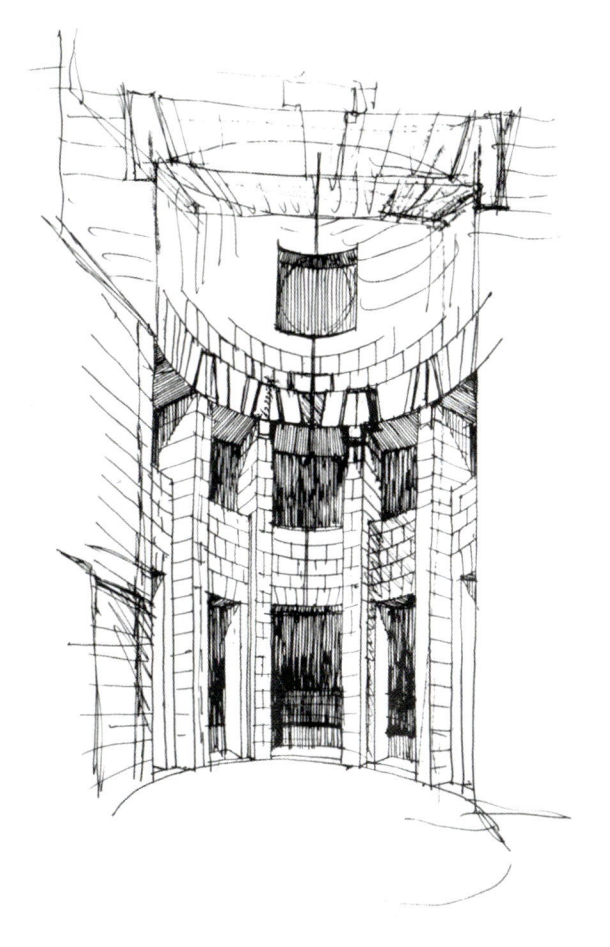

Right:
Pedestrian axis through the Supreme Court to the Knesset

Left:
Balconies of the judges' chambers facing west

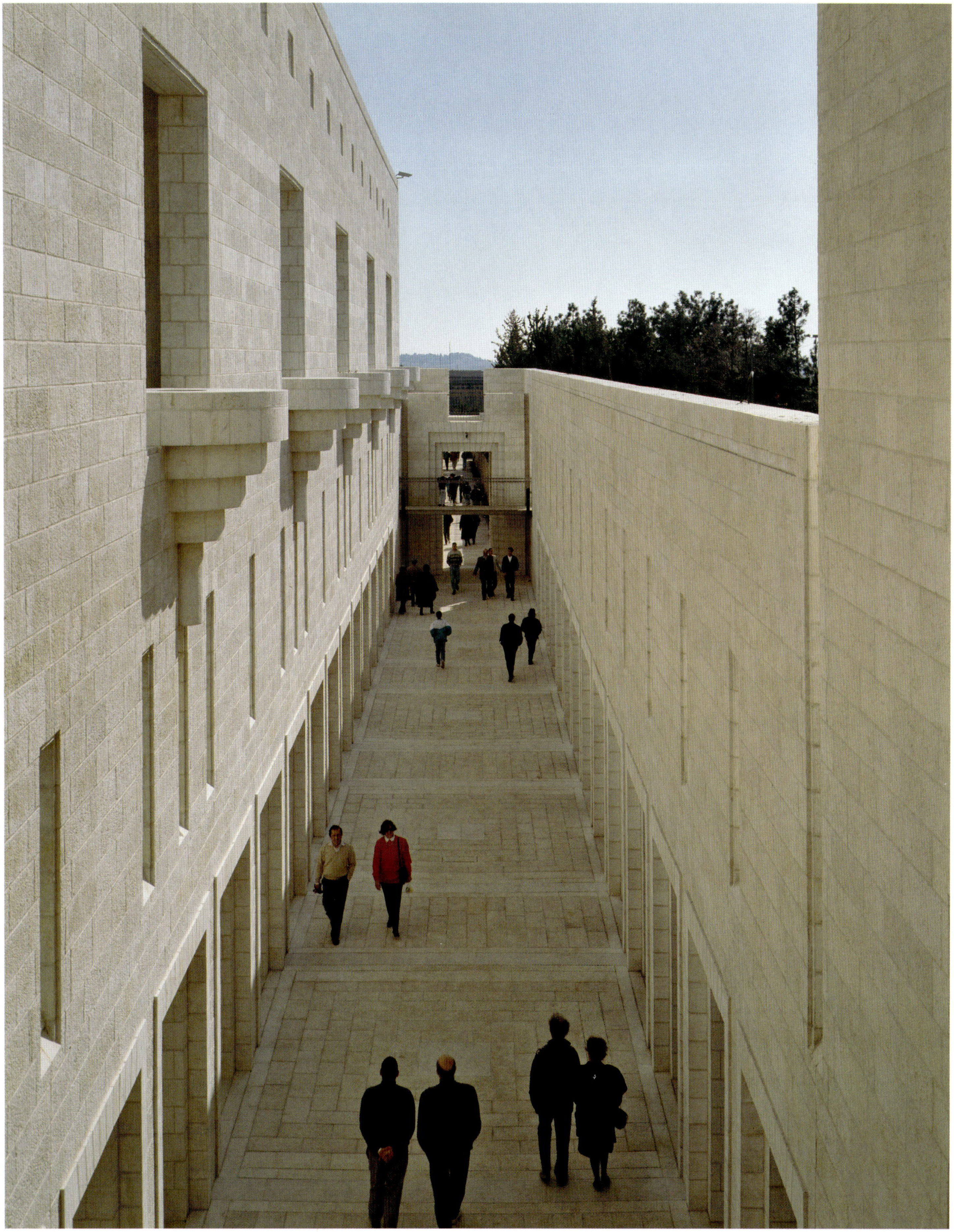

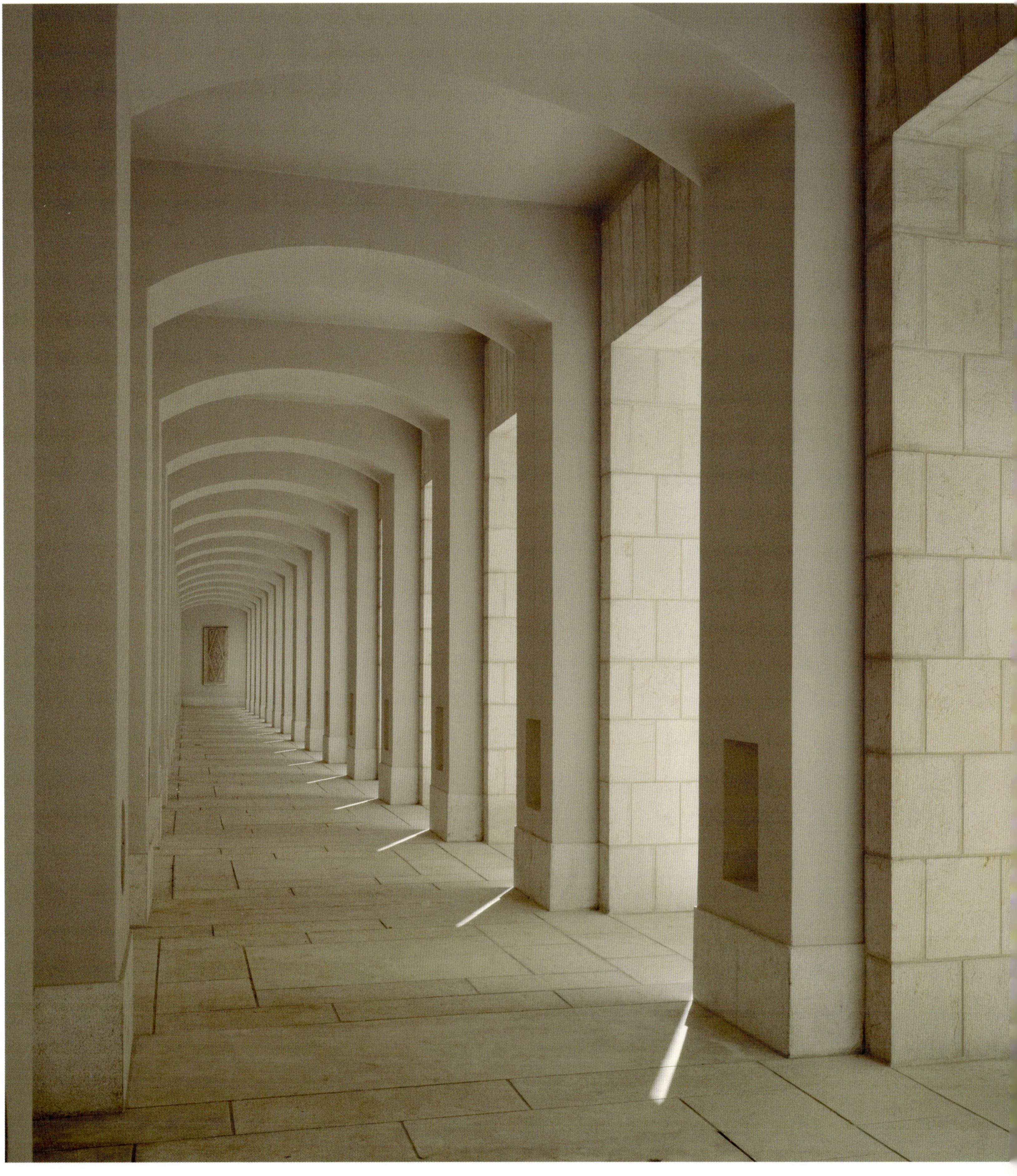

Pedestrian arcade leading to the Knesset

96

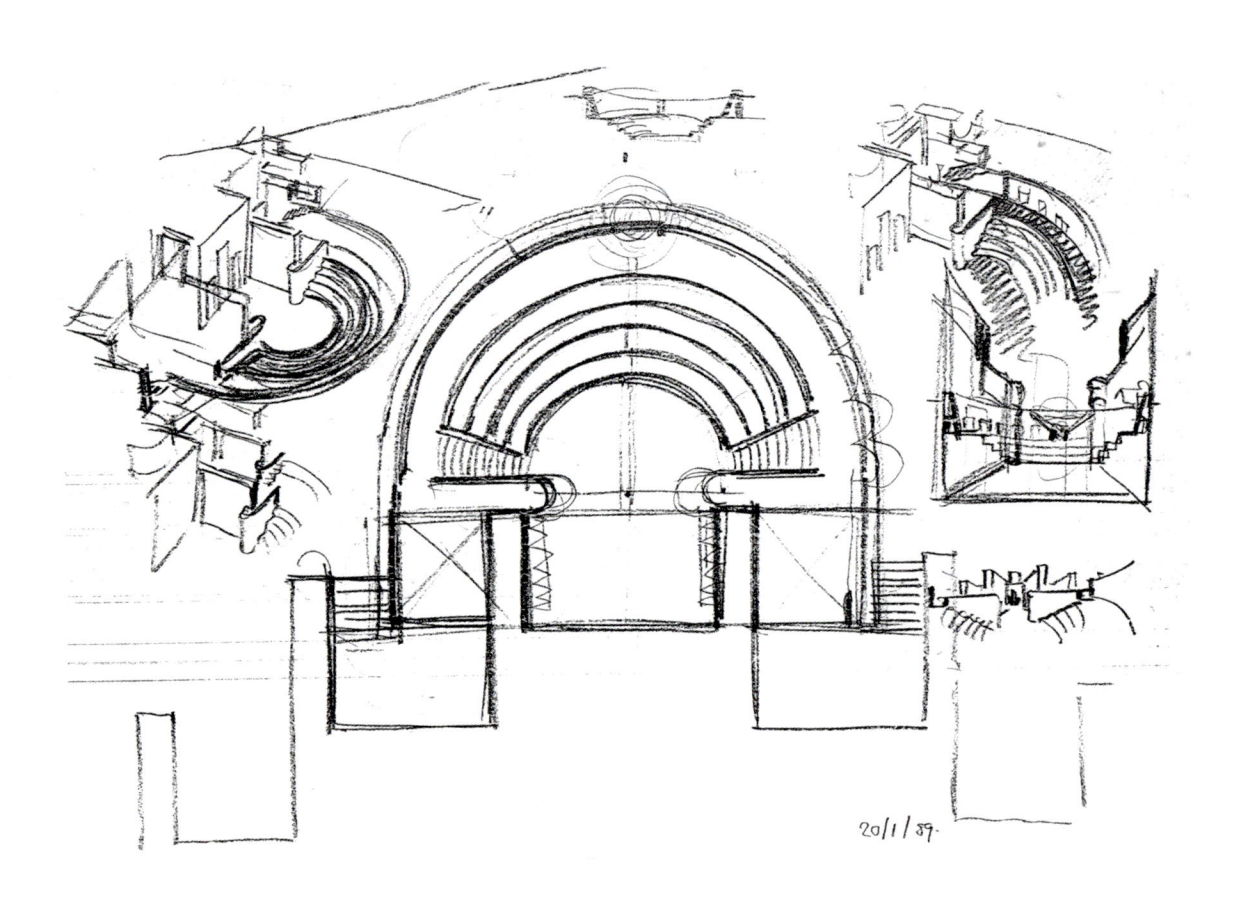

Left:
Sketch: sunken courtyard

Left below:
The central courtroom, the cafeteria below and the sunken courtyard

Right:
South elevation

South elevation

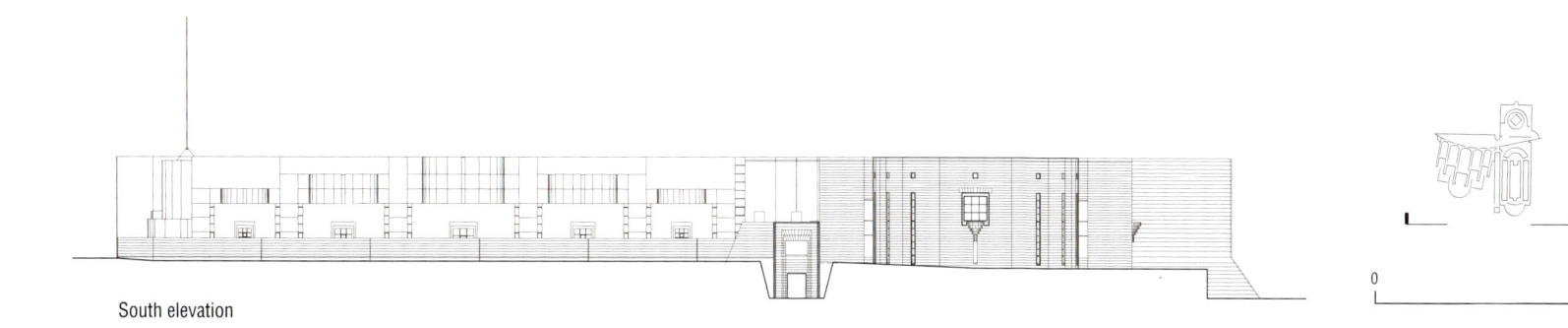

0  25 M

Above:
East elevation

Left:
Cantilevered balcony facing Jerusalem

Right:
West elevation

West elevation (A)

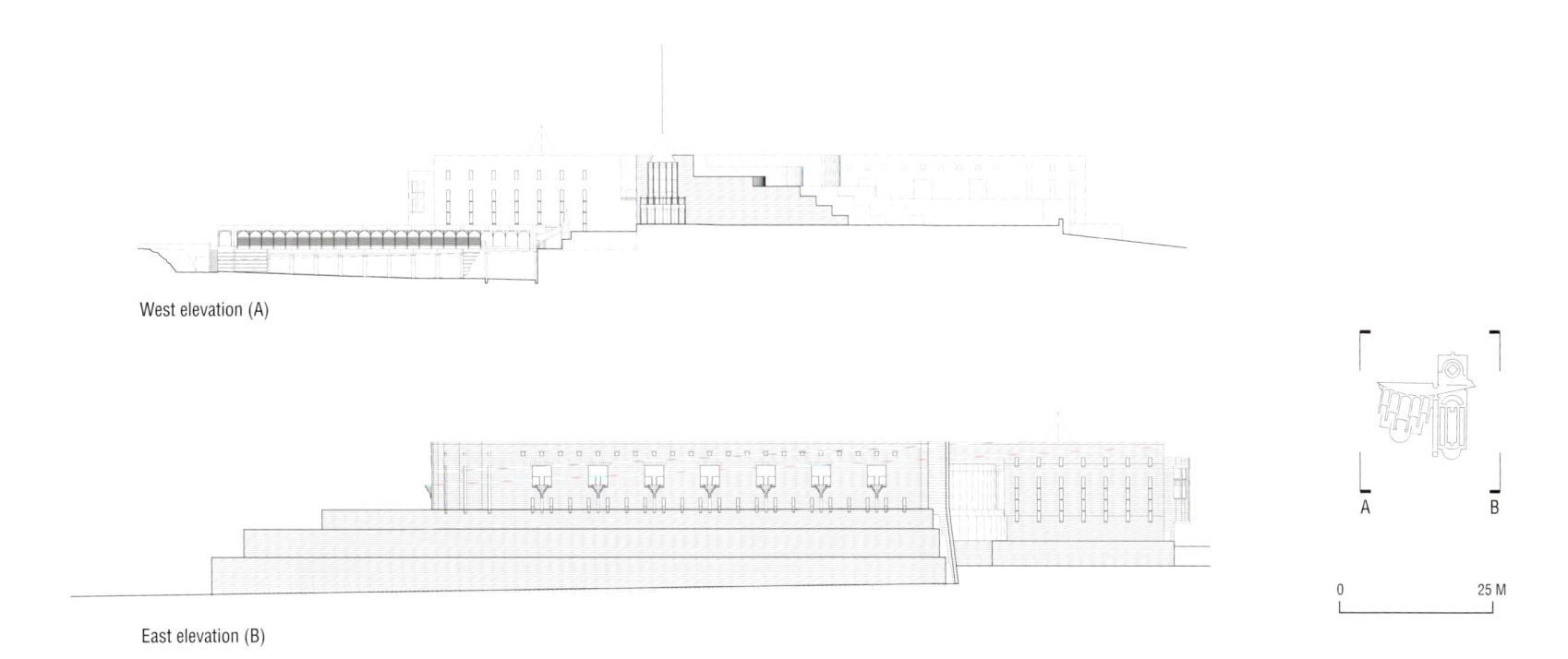

East elevation (B)

0    25 M

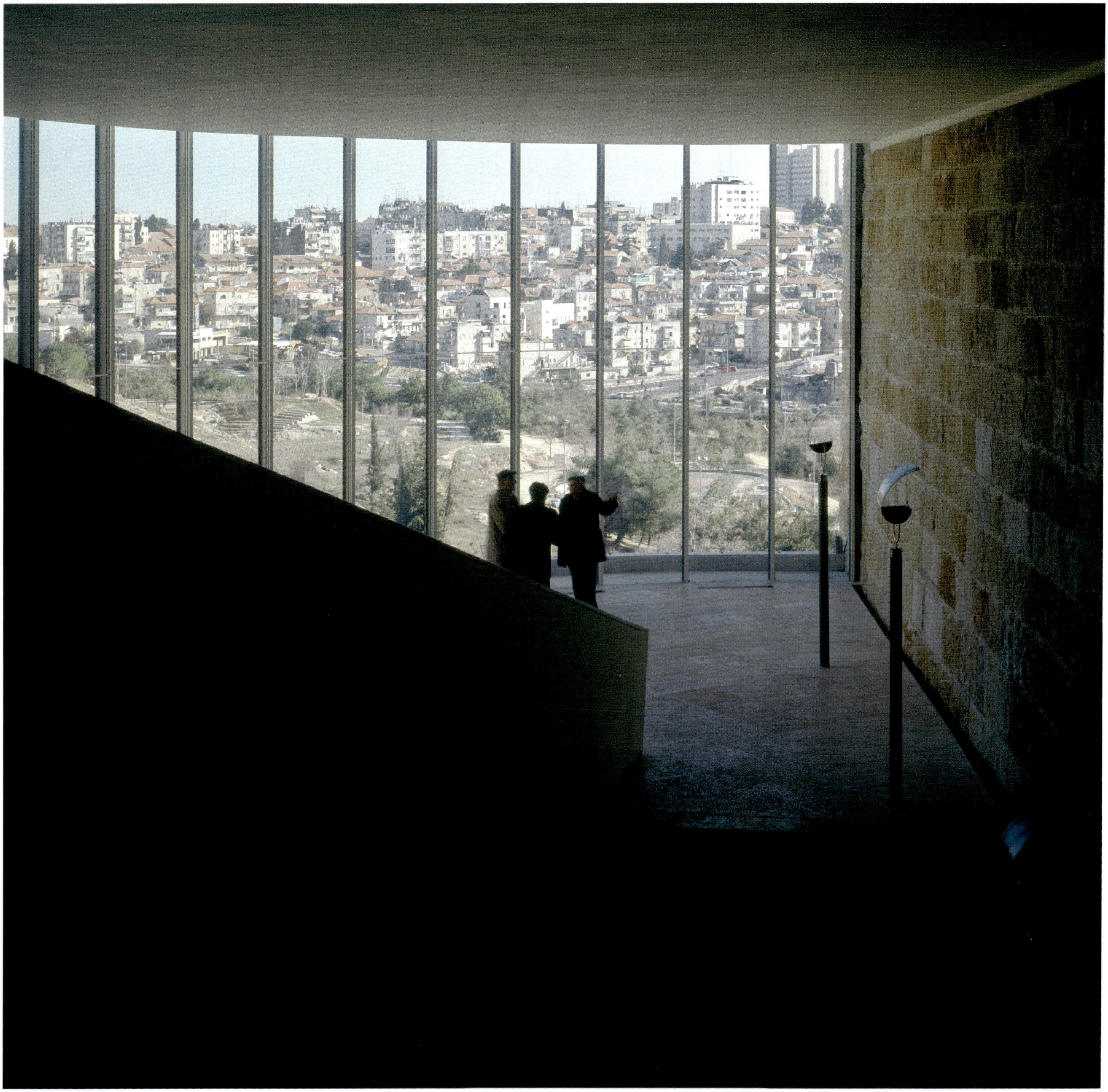

Right:
View of main entrance, stairs to judges' level

Below right:
Sketch: public stairway leading to the window and the 'Tent'

Left:
Stairway up to the public foyer

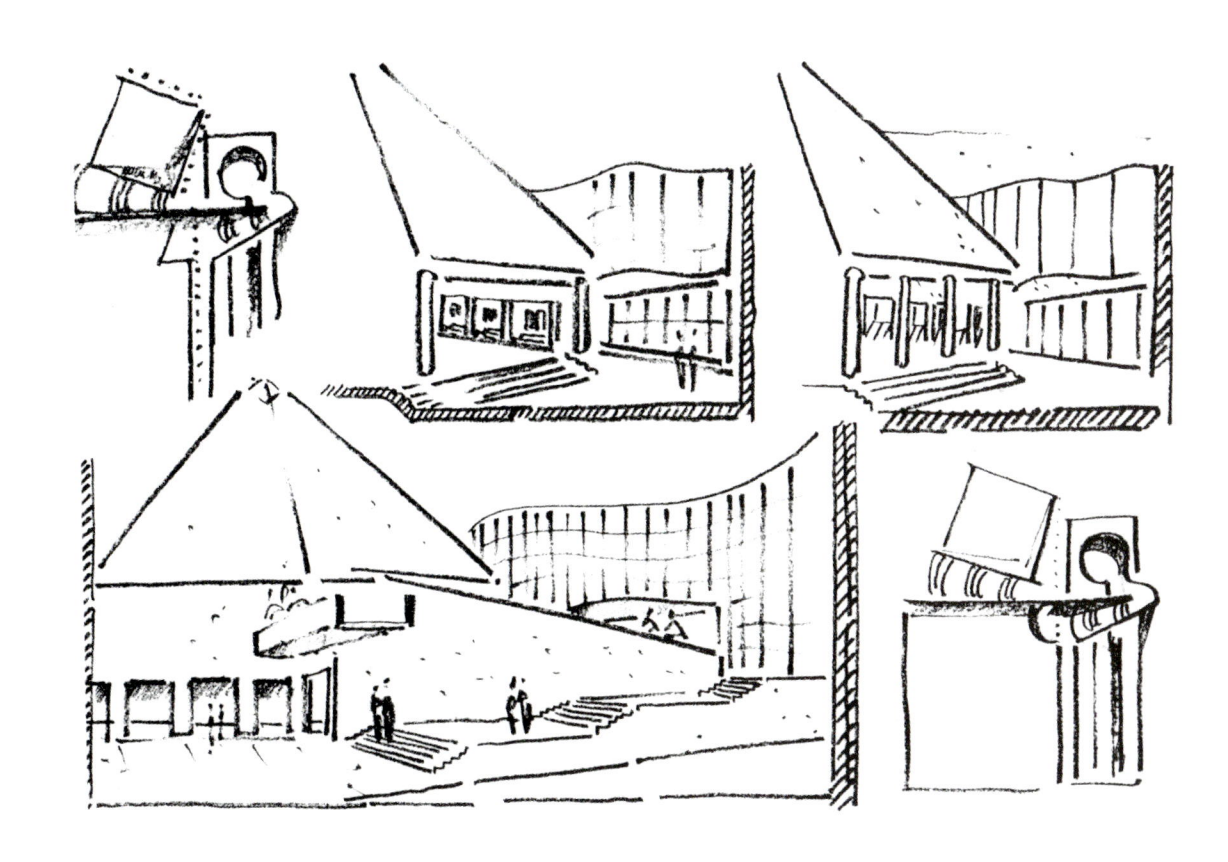

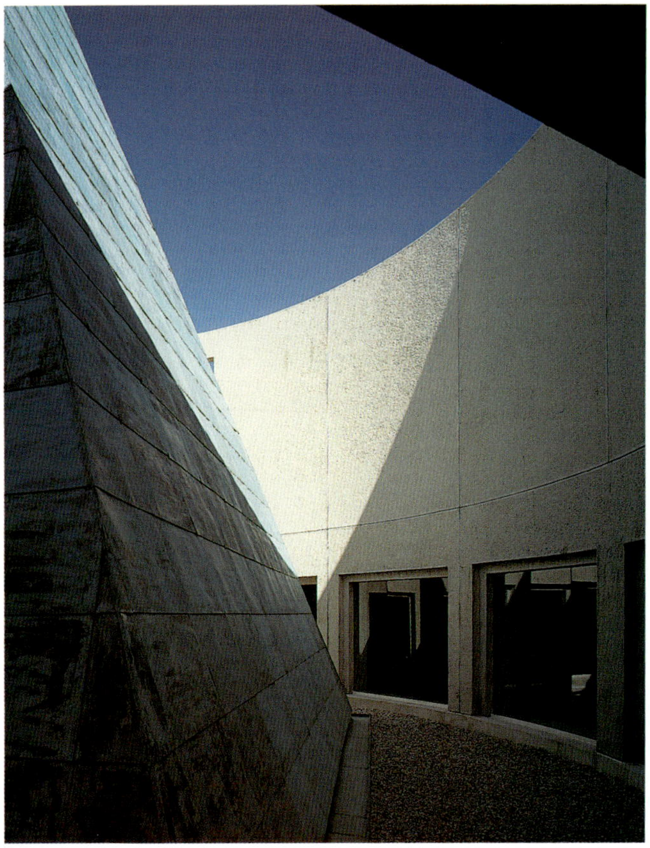

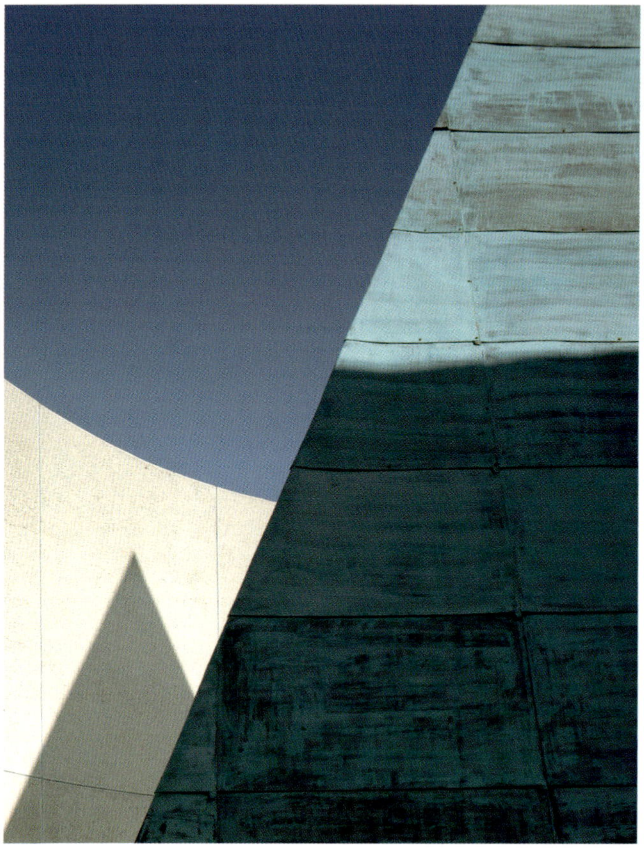

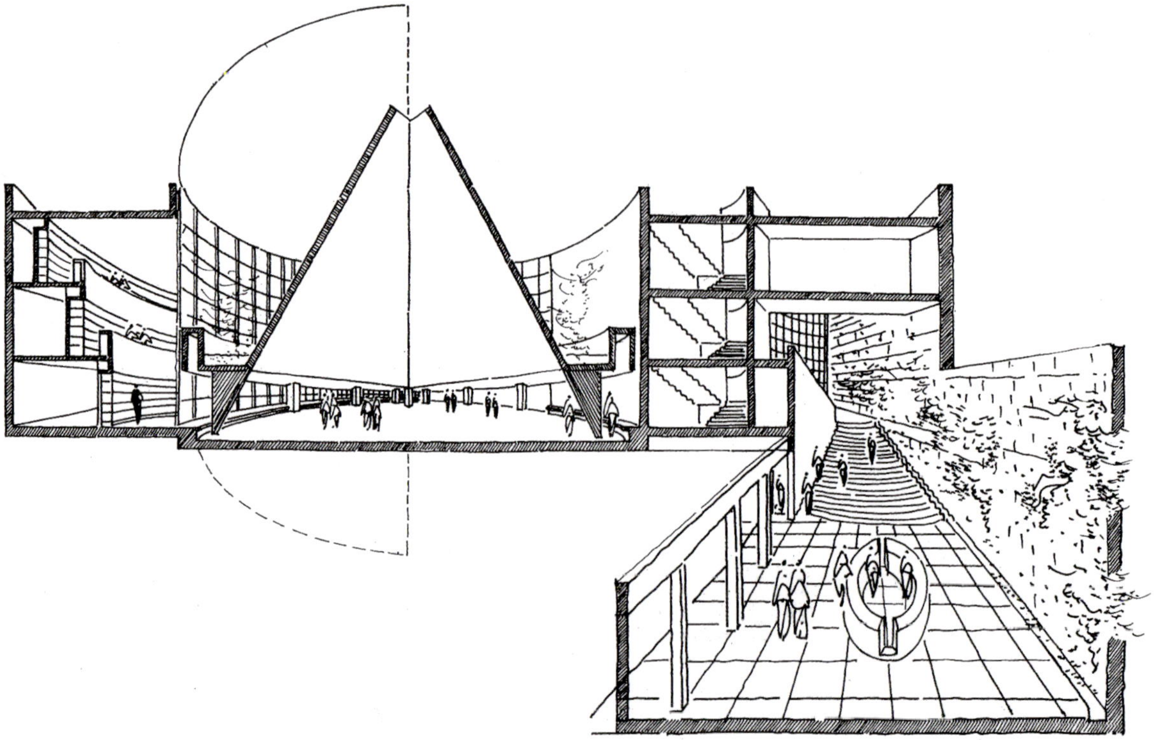

Right:
Natural light filtering into the interior of the 'Tent' through four 'lenses'

Left above:
The external space between the 'Tent' and the surrounding library

Left below:
The main entrance, the stairway, the window, the 'Tent', and the surrounding library

The Supreme Court library lit from the external courtyard

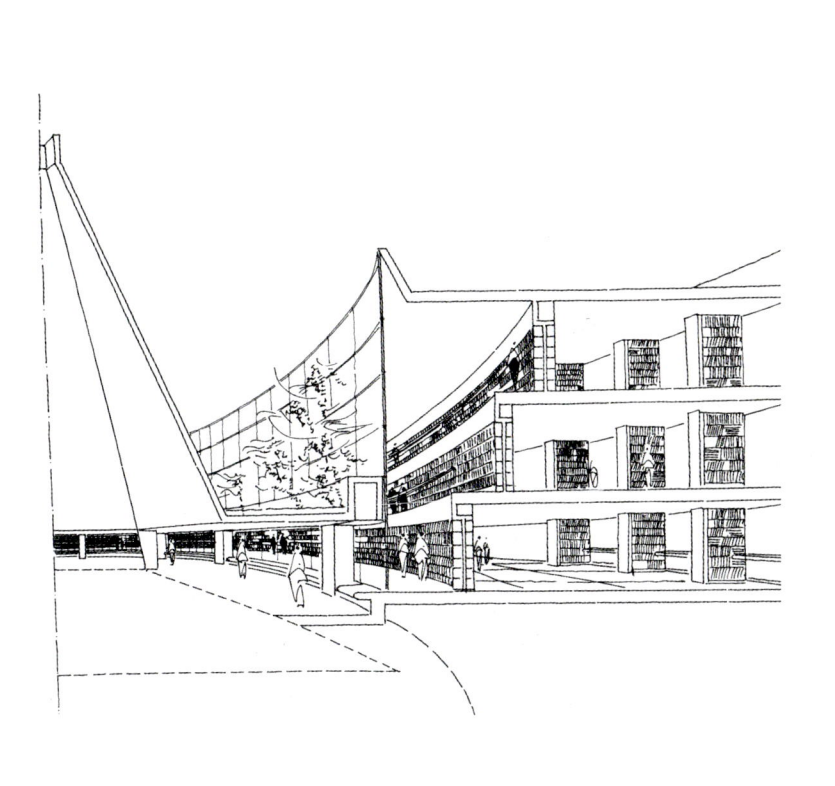

Above:
Stairs to the judges' level
within the library

Below:
Sketch: the cascading
bookshelves

Lightwell over the
waiting area

Right:
The main public foyer,
the waiting areas and the
entries to the courtrooms

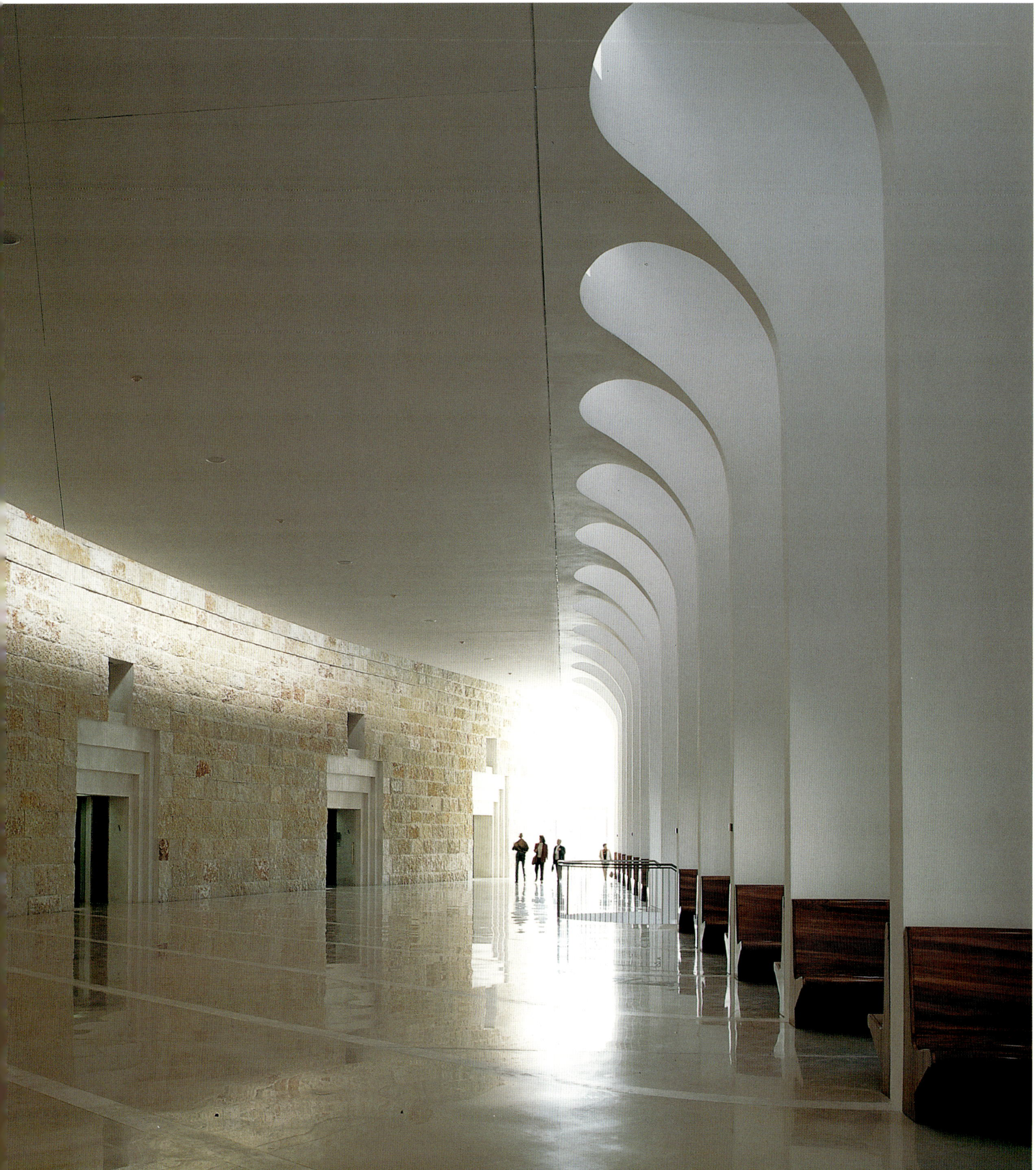

Left:
Lightwells over the waiting area

Right above:
Detail of the cylinders inserted between the concrete ceiling and the hung ceiling for indirect light over the alcoves

Right below:
Waiting area, indirect light and reflections

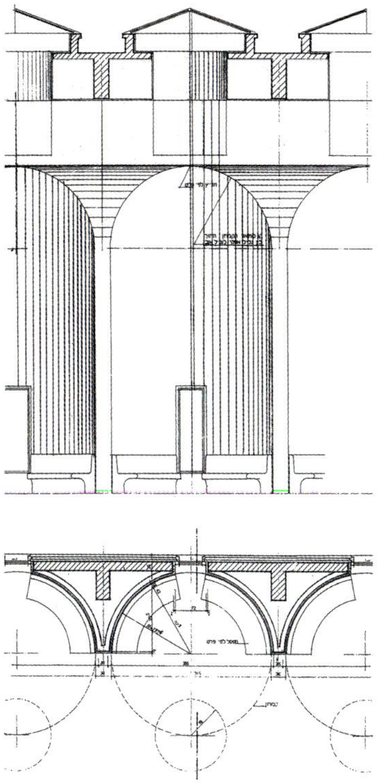

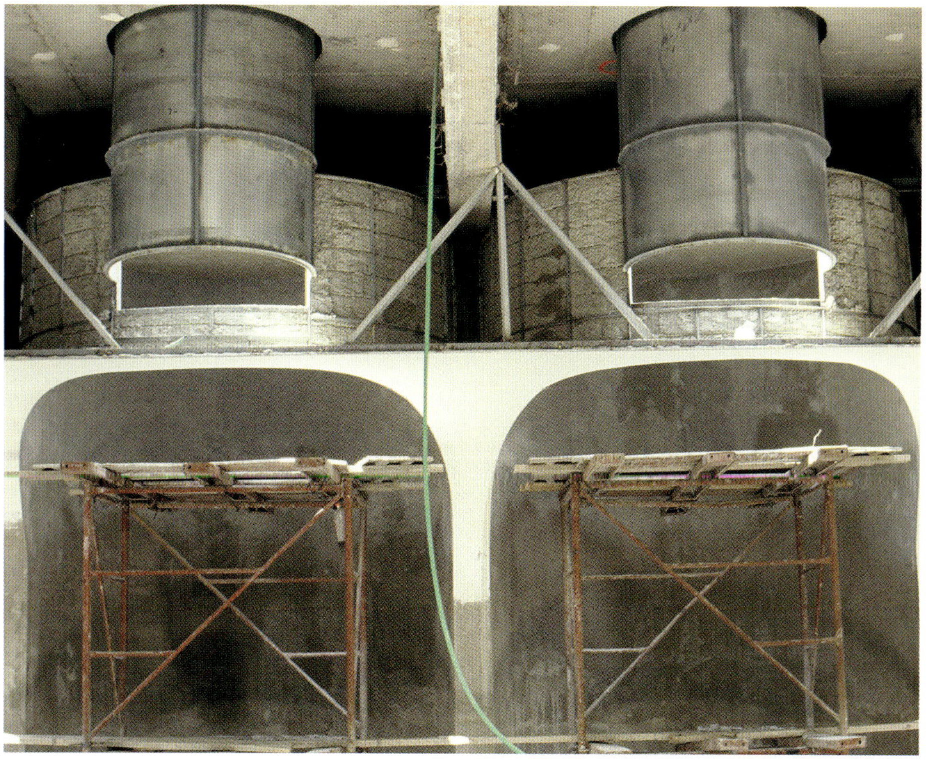

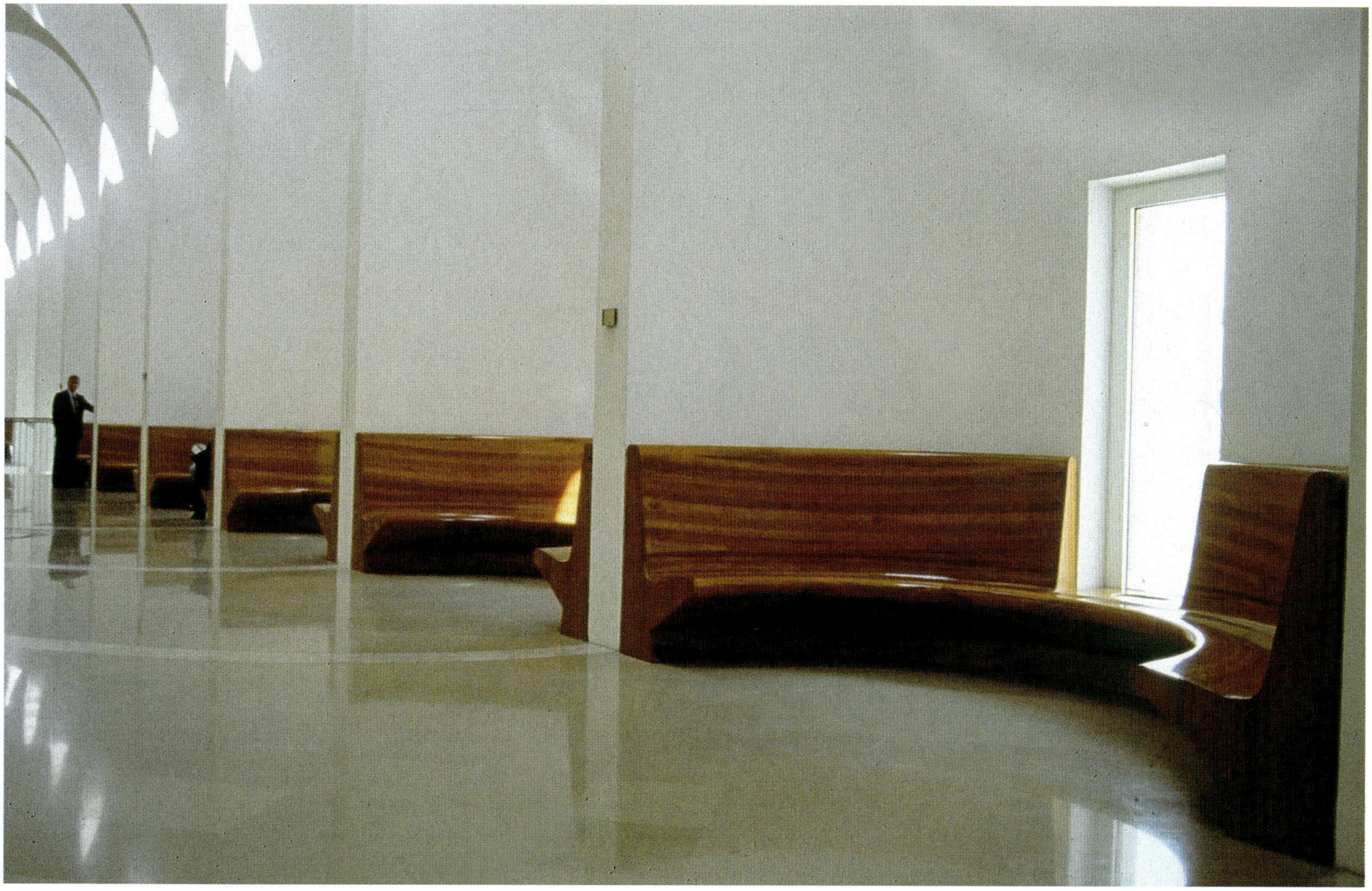

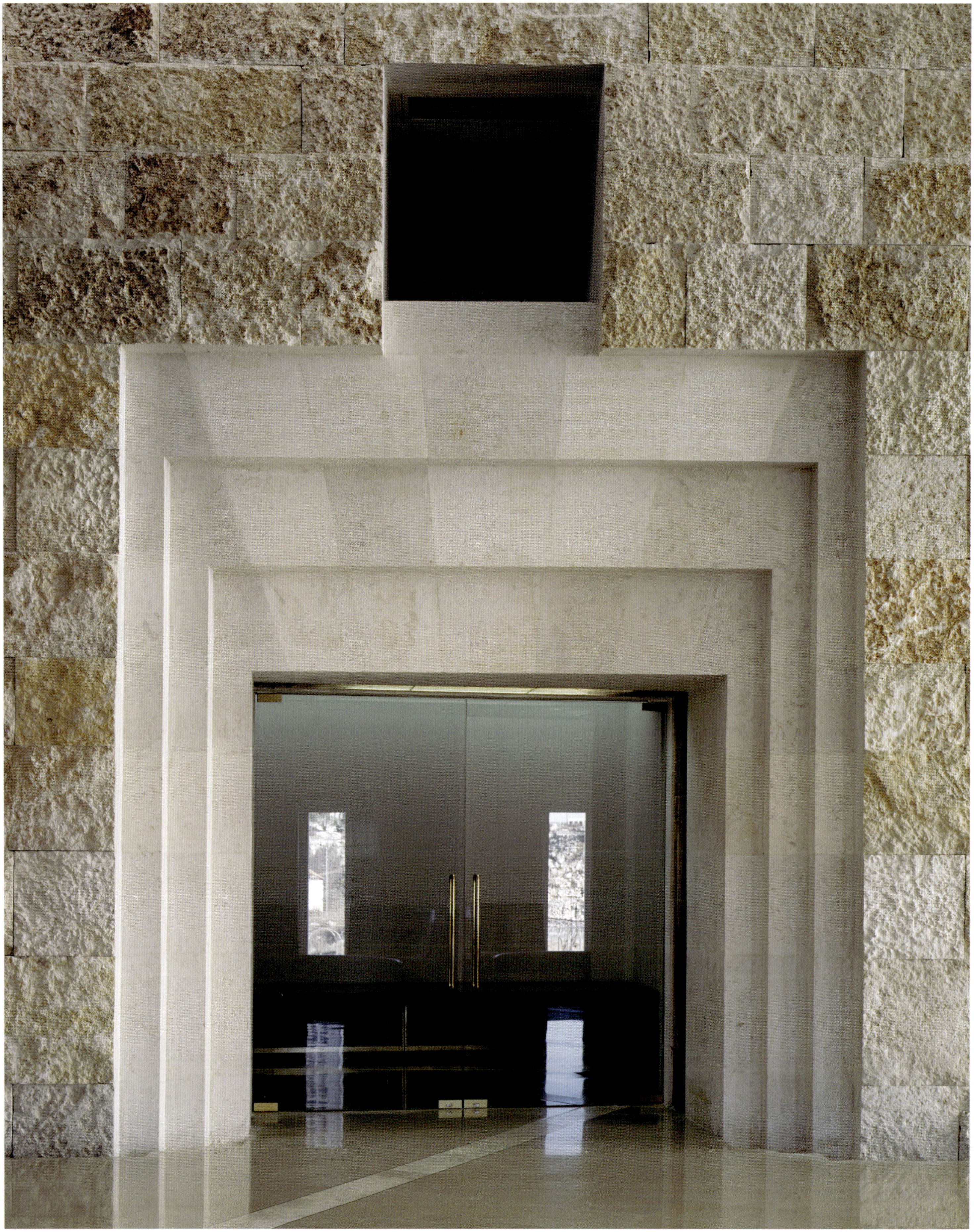

Left:
'Gate' to the main courtroom

Right:
Indirect light bouncing into the courtroom

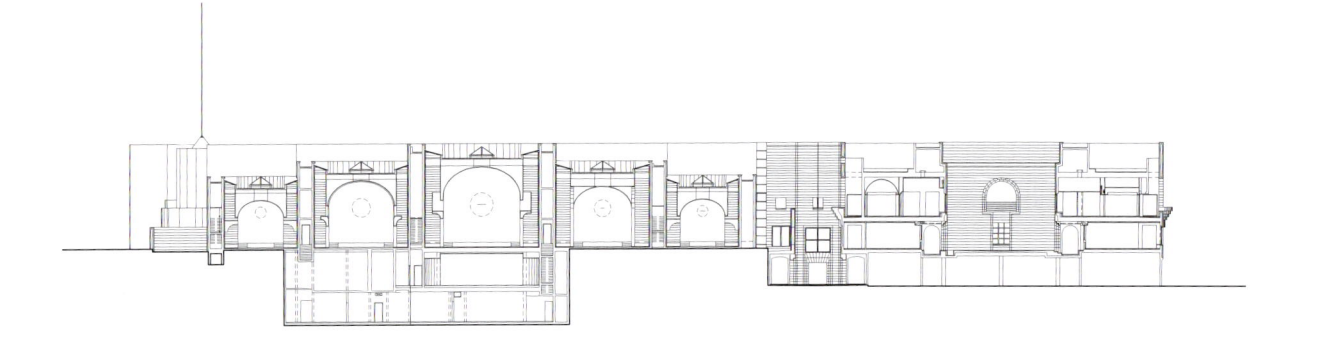

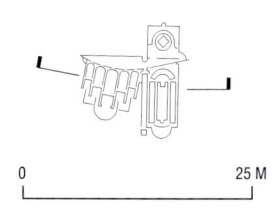

East–west section through courtrooms and administration

The main courtroom

Right:
The small courtroom

Left:
Sketch: the indirect light over the sidewalls of the courtrooms

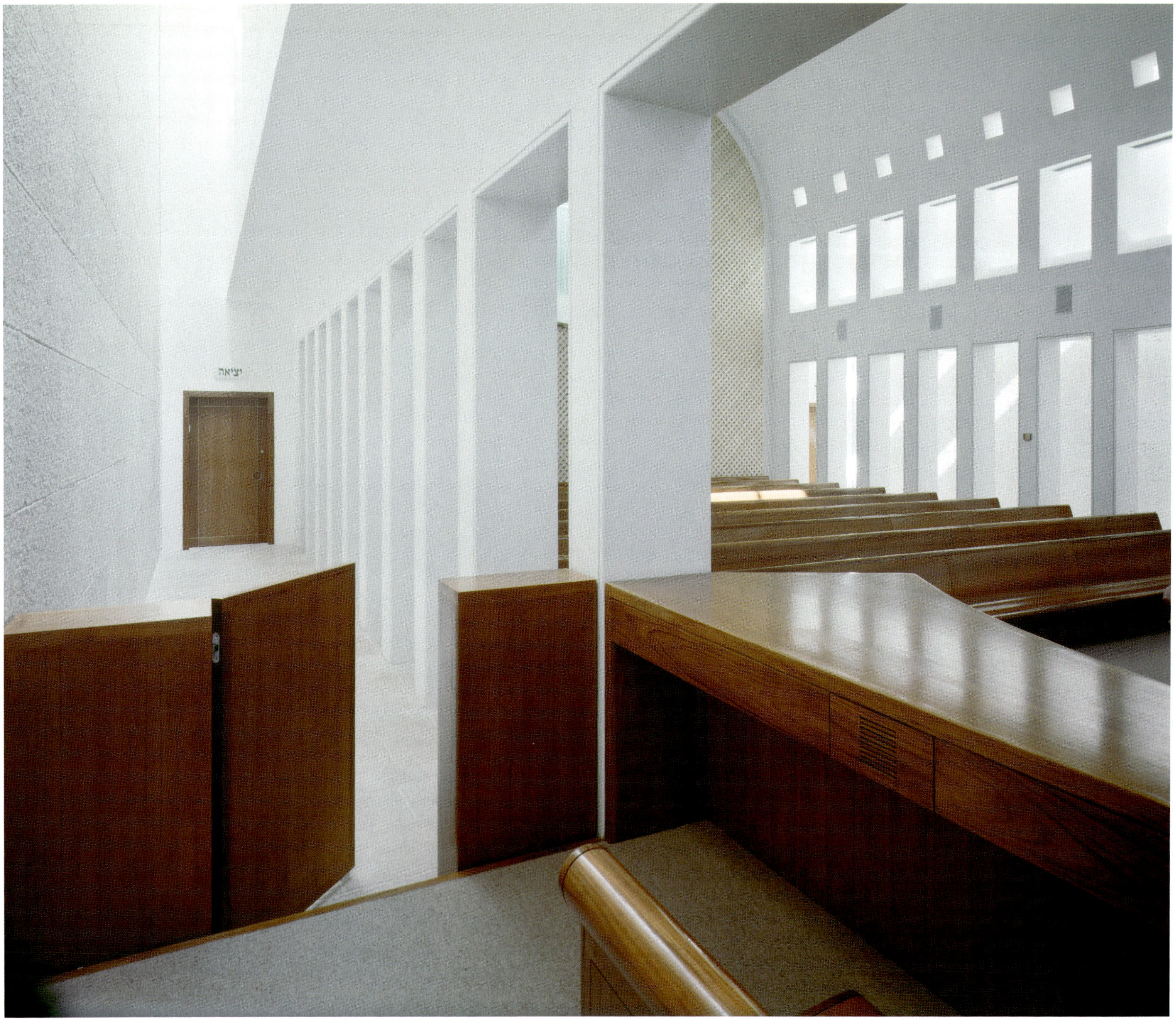
יציאה

Side aisles with indirect light bouncing into the courtroom

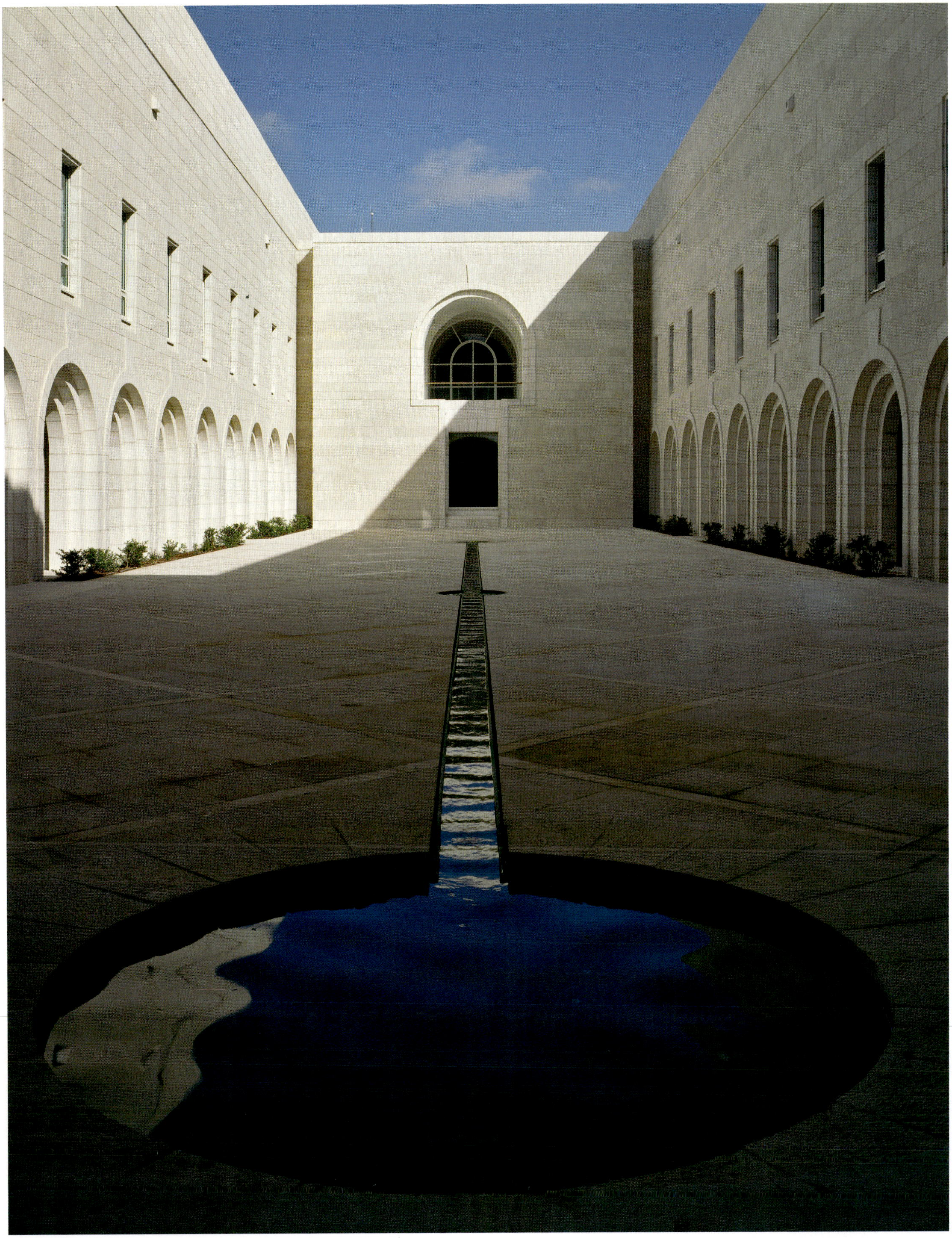

Left:
Detail: the copper water channel

Right:
The judges' courtyard

Left:
The Arcade surrounding the Courtyard

Right:
A view towards the Courtyard from the Administrative Offices on the Ground Level

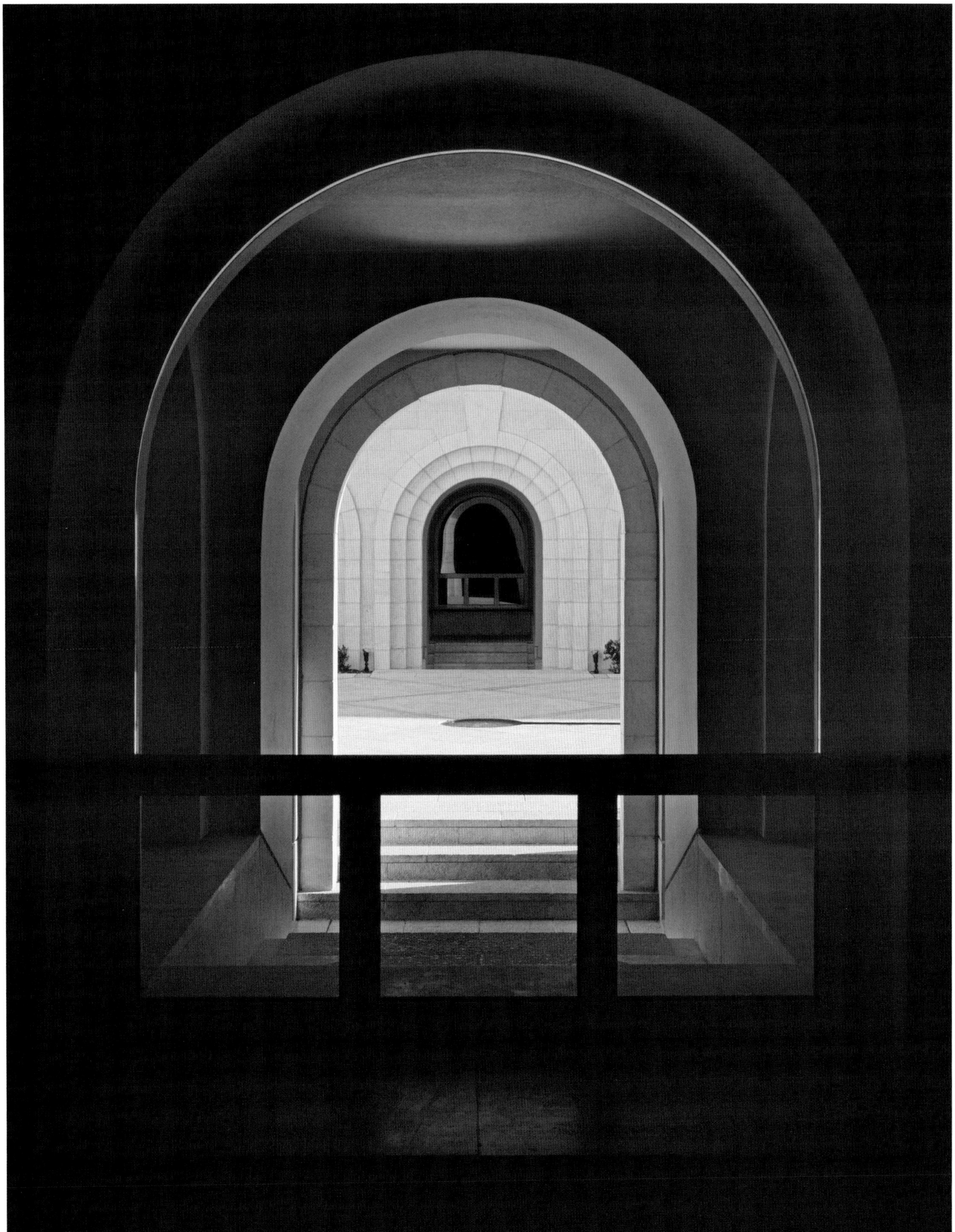

Above:
The judges' dining area

Right:
A view towards the
courtyard from the
administrative offices

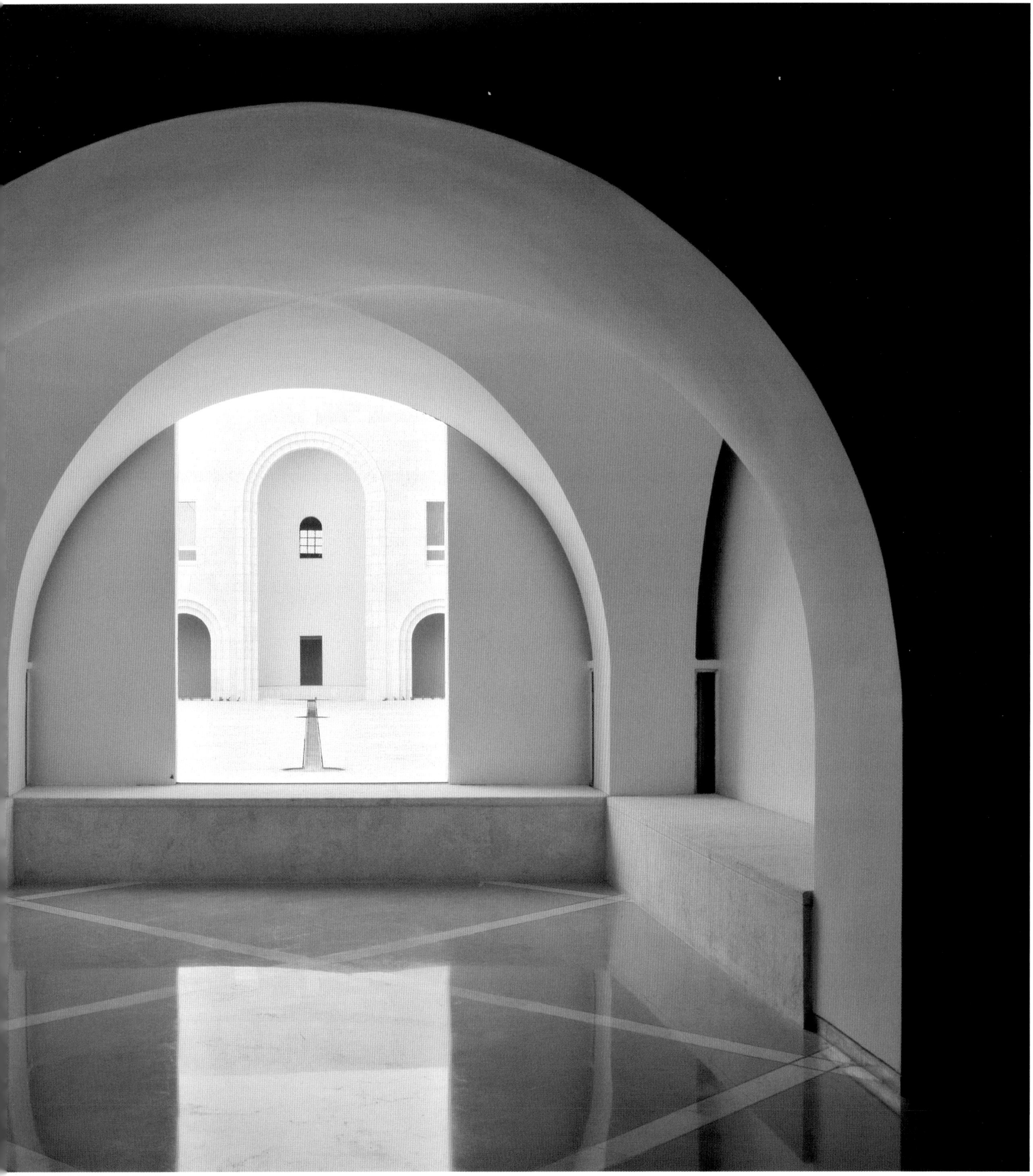

Left:
Small conference room

Right:
Main conference room

Opposite:
The Chief Justice's chamber

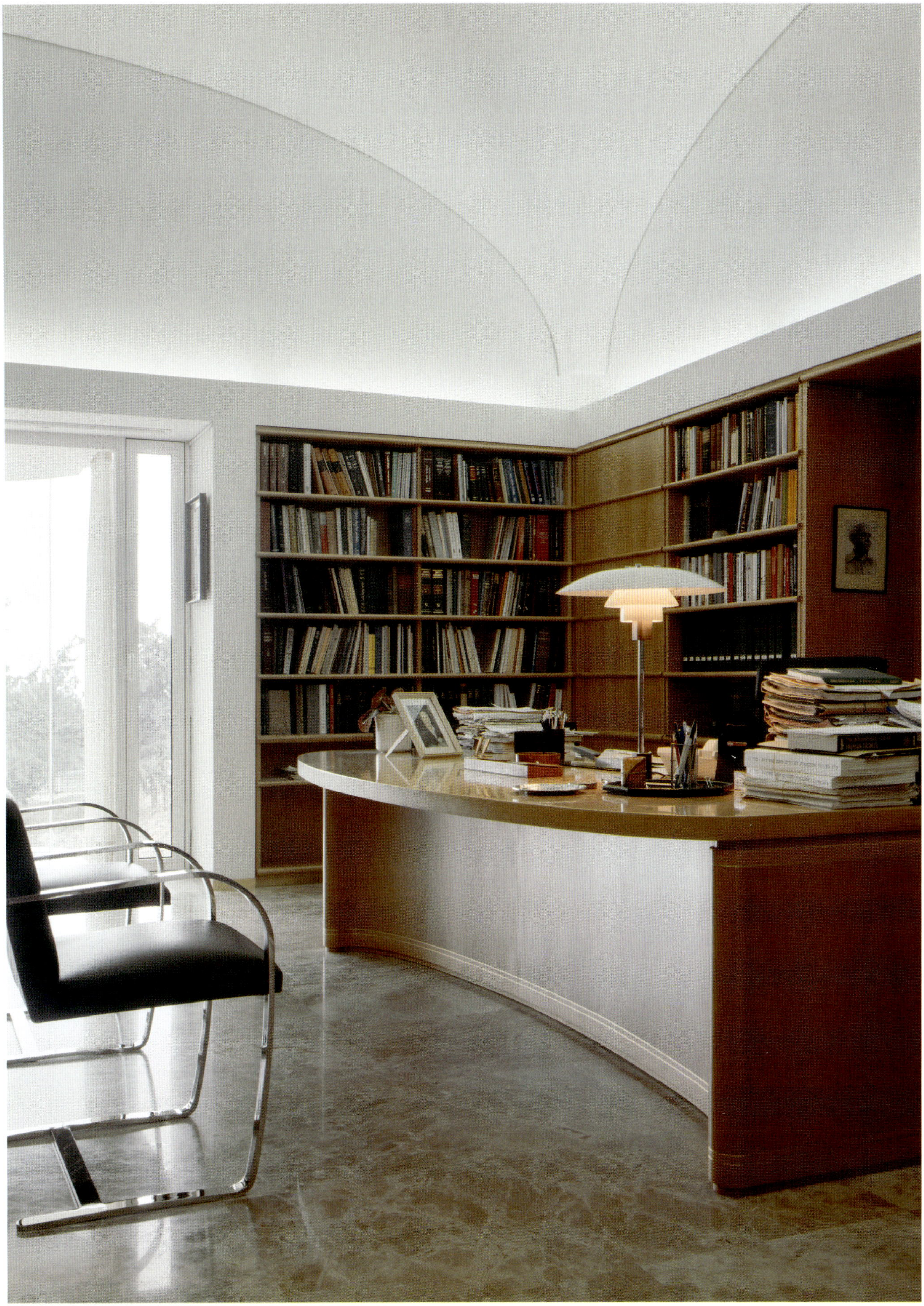

Stone, metal, wood, copper and light details

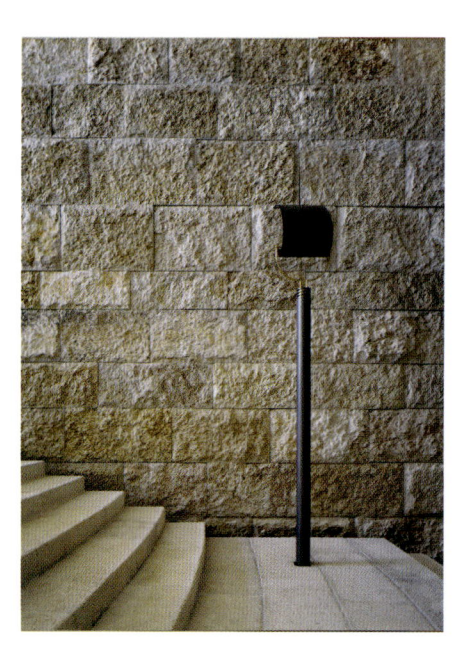

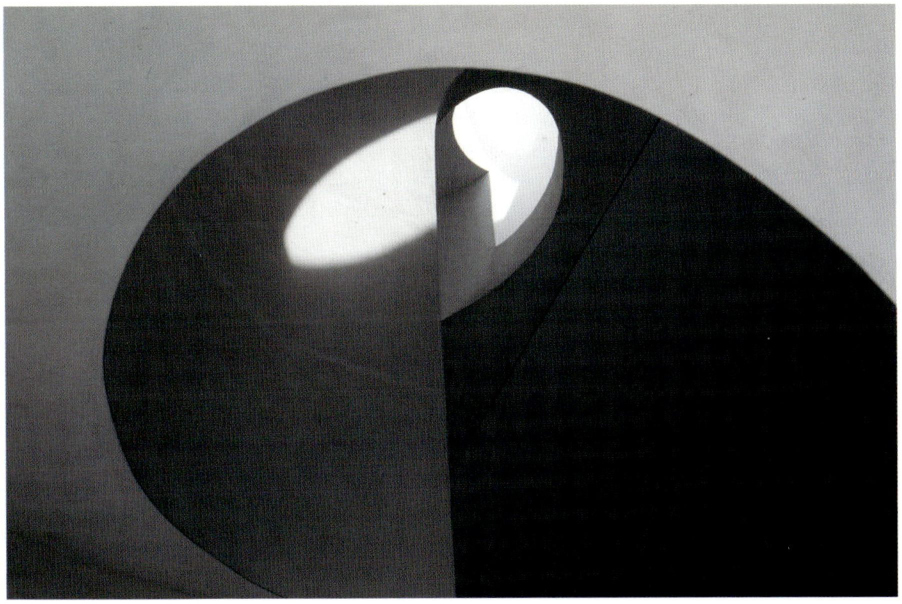

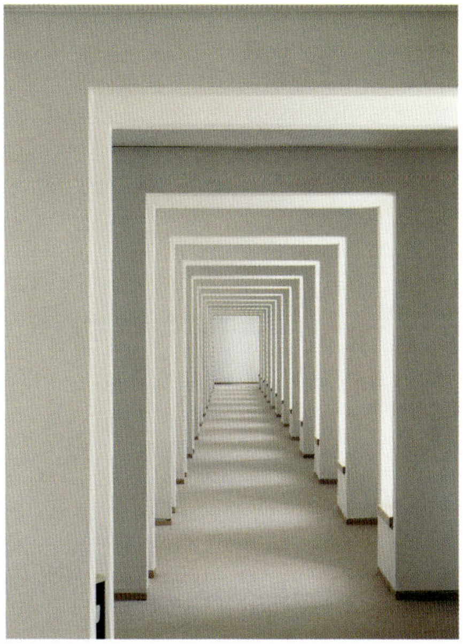

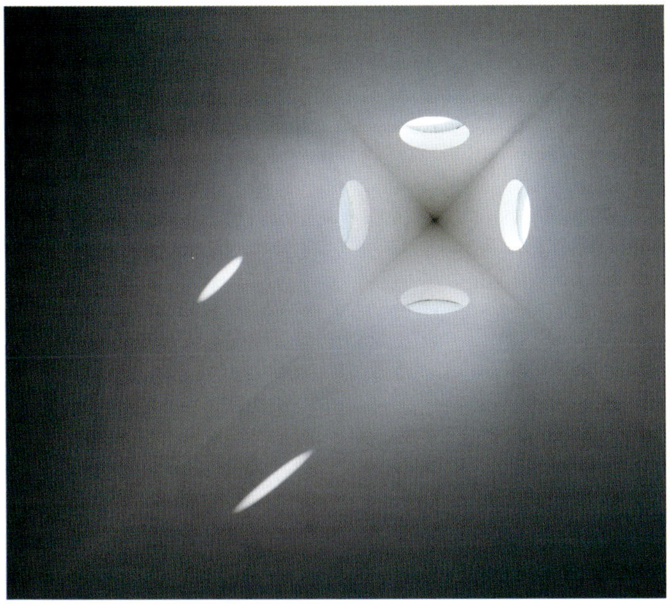

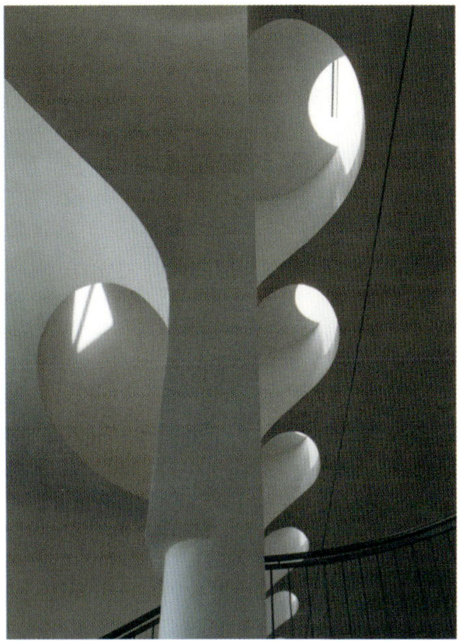

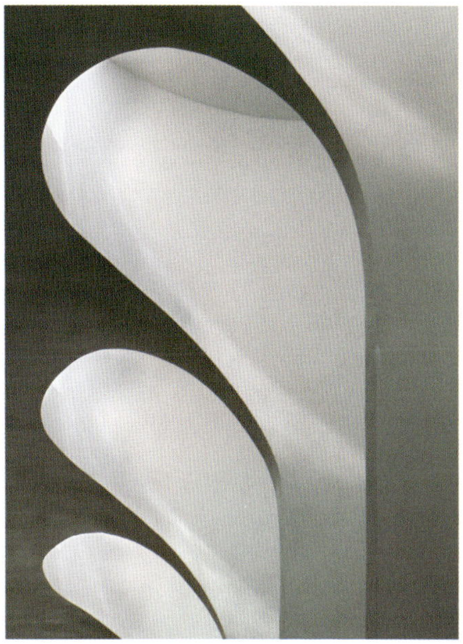

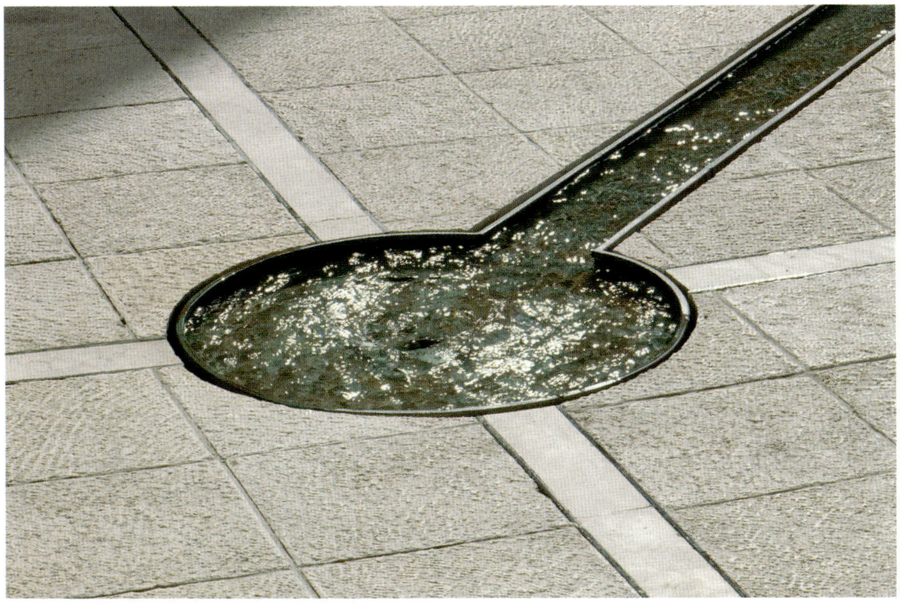

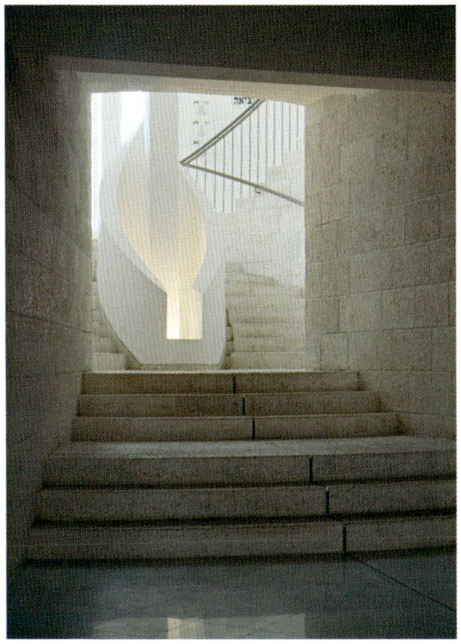

# Epilogue

Ada Karmi-Melamede

My work is influenced by the language of local architecture that preceded it in this region – by the Christian and Islamic architecture of the late-nineteenth century, the 'white architecture' of the British Mandate (1917–48), and the Brutalist architecture of the late 1950s. Until the first years of the twentieth century, local architecture was primarily characterized by load-bearing stone construction. The weight and thickness of the walls provided protection as well as acoustic and climatic insulation. The limitations inherent in stone construction determined the size and nature of all openings and the structural spans of the buildings. Buildings descended heavily to the ground. They were introspective with rich spatial compositions in both plan and section.

Towards the end of the twentieth century, a new technologically informed global architectonic language developed. Through the use of reinforced concrete, steel, glass and an array of new and lighter materials and ever-more-sophisticated joints between materials, exterior skins developed that were lighter, more flexible, more transparent, and entirely self supported – *independent* of the building's interiors. In Israel, this development was not as widespread or sophisticated due to the market size. The newest materials were not easily accessible, nor was the technological expertise.

From a social perspective, the multiculturalism of this country (historically and now), constant political and social struggles, frequent wars, and the ideological utopianism of a new society that was and is no more, have all left their stamp on Israeli architecture's substance and form. The paucity of local materials and production capabilities, the topography, the intense fluctuations of light and shadow, and the limited supply of water, vegetation and shade have also influenced trends and shaped any imported architectonic concepts. All of these factors are still present to this day.

My work tends to exist between extremes – it is often heavy on the outside, 'flexing' its roots, while much more free and individualistic on the inside. In such an intense, ever-changing place, where history, present and future, are unusually loaded, the search for the character of an 'Israeli architecture' is particularly challenging.

The three projects in this volume were commissioned by an extraordinary client. Each project came with challenging symbolic questions about weighty issues of law, justice, education, memory and community – to name just a few. Each came with a complex and ambitious program and they each occupied uniquely defining sites. The Supreme Court building, won after a daunting international competition, is in an area called Government Hill, facing Parliament; The Open University is the largest university in the country that operates by correspondence and is located on the very edge of a city facing a regional highway; Ramat Hanadiv's Visitors Centre faces the Rothschild Memorial Gardens on a hill overlooking the Mediterranean and the Carmel range on one of the most breathtaking sites in the country.

All three buildings are layered and introspective. Each one establishes strong connections with the landscape and/or the urban fabric beyond. In each, an attempt has been made to delineate a space that was representative of the public scale without compromising the private one. They are all dressed in concrete and stone. They descend forcefully to the ground and carve the topography beneath and beside them. The different levels inside and outside the buildings change the users' connection with the landscape, modify visual perspectives and blur the physical boundaries of these buildings – aiming to enrich the relationships within and without. All three buildings contain combinations of contained and flowing spaces. Walkways have a strong presence and even their own architecture. Beyond being places for people to walk, they are places for people to meet and linger; places for light and shadow to interact; and places where building structure can be experienced. The movement of people, the transitions of light and the structural rhythm merge in these spaces and form the dynamic pulse of the building.

Despite being elusive, amorphous, and in a state of continuous change, natural light is the most available, magical and inexpensive building material in Israel. Light can shape, colour, harden, soften, and sculpt architecture – it offers tremendous dimensions of freedom and serendipity. Light suggests what lies beyond function and invites itself to visit the architecture.

At its best, architecture creates a place in which the personal and individual dimensions connect with something greater. Regardless of current trends and technological innovations, it is imperative to keep questioning what one should remember from the past and what one should forget; what one should embrace from the new and what one should preserve; and why. I am drawn to the tension that exists between the elements of architecture that pull us upwards and outside of ourselves, those that keep us in the moment, and those that draw us back into history. It is the interaction and balance between these that creates a spirit of place.

On a personal note, I would like to thank Yad Hanadiv in general and Dorothy de Rothschild, Jacob Rothschild, Arthur Fried, Ariel Weiss and the amazing staff of the Foundation specifically, for giving me the opportunity to work on such extraordinary, varied and beautiful projects. I am deeply grateful for the support, intelligence, commitment and enthusiasm that was brought to the table each and every time.

*Toda raba raba – Ada Karmi-Melamede*

**Credits:**

### The Supreme Court Building

**Client**:
Yad Hanadiv

**Architect**:
Karmi Architects, Ltd.
Ram Karmi
Ada Karmi Melamede

**Project Architect**:
Meir Drezner

**Design Team:** Iftach Issacharov, Simon Friedman, Alan Aronoff, Ruth Rotholtz Van Eick, Daniel Azerrad, Moty Shyovitz, Rami Yogev, Tzadik Eliakim, Zvi Dunsky, Dan Price, and Tal Gazit

**Photographer**: Richard Bryant

----

### The Open University

**Client**:
Yad Hanadiv

**Architect**:
Ada Karmi Melamede Architects
Ada Karmi Melamede

**Project Architect**:
Amit Nemlich

**Design Team**: Ori Rotem, Tal Zakut, Michal Shefer, Shiri Peretz, Sharon Harari, Zvi Gersh, Sharon Paz, Yuval Amitzi, Dalia Nachman-Farchi, Dani Dinari, Roy Seker

**Photographer**: Richard Bryant / Ardon Bar-Hama

----

### Ramat Hanadiv Visiting Center

**Client**:
Yad Hanadiv

**Architect**:
Ada Karmi Melamede Architects
Ada Karmi Melamede

**Project Architect**: Guy Teomi, Yuval Amitzi

**Design Team**: Dror Hai, Michal Shefer, Dalia Nachman-Farchi

**Photographer**: Amit Geron